TIVERTON &
LITTLE COMPTON

RHODE ISLAND

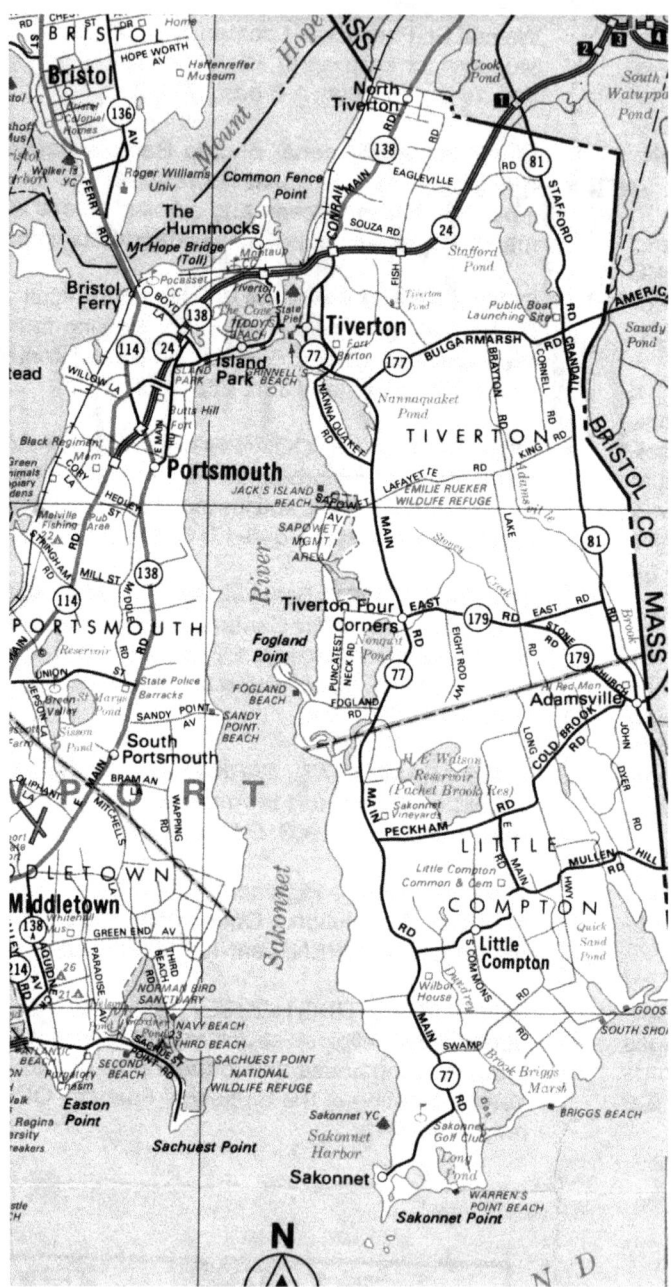

This section of an official State of Rhode Island highway map affords the reader a bird's-eye perspective of Tiverton and Little Compton's locations on the Sakonnet River and their proximity to Portsmouth on Aquidneck Island. The reader can appreciate the unobstructed view from Fort Barton across the narrow divide of the Sakonnet to the Portsmouth site of the Battle of Rhode Island.

TIVERTON &
LITTLE COMPTON

RHODE ISLAND

HISTORIC TALES OF THE
OUTER PLANTATIONS

Richard V. Simpson

THE
History
PRESS

Published by The History Press
Charleston, SC 29403
www.historypress.net

Front cover image is a postcard issued by the Little Compton Historical Society. Back cover image is a circa 1910 postcard showing a pogy boat in the Sakonnet River, with the Old Stone Bridge in the background.

All images are from the author's collection unless otherwise noted.

First published 2012

ISBN 978.1.5402.3238.0

Library of Congress CIP data applied for.

This volume is dedicated to all Native Americans who fought and died for their country.

In recognition of Native Americans' sensitivity about the word "squaw" when used by nonnatives in reference to Indian women, in this narrative I have substituted the word "female" where one usually reads "squaw."

CONTENTS

Preface   9

Introduction   11

Tiverton: A Historical Prospective   15

Architectural and Historical Landmarks   32

Stone Bridge and Stone Bridge Inn   38

The Railroad   50

Colonel Barton and the Battle of Rhode Island   60

Bridgeport and Nannaquaket   68

A House Called Nannaquaket   72

Four Corners and the Old Whipping Post   77

Sin and Flesh Brook   89

Little Compton: A Historical Prospective   96

Town Churches and Public Schools   104

Captain Benjamin Church   114

Around the Commons   120

Adamsville and Spite Tower   124

The Appeal of Being Remote   128

Sydney Richmond Burleigh, Artist   141

CONTENTS

A Little Compton Timeline   145

Glossary of Wampanoag Indian Words   151

Notes   153

Bibliography   157

About the Author   159

PREFACE

The objective of this narrative is to present brief but compelling sketches of some of the most significant personalities, momentous events and architectural resources existing in the historical record of Rhode Island's outlying plantations, Tiverton and Little Compton.

To old-time, longtime residents and their families, some of these recollections may seem redundant, but to new residents and vacationing visitors, these stories will be novel and refreshingly interesting.

This isolated stretch of Rhode Island, from the beginning of occupancy by English colonists in the mid-1600s, is thought to have originally included the Aquidneck Island towns of Portsmouth, Tiverton and Little Compton, Rhode Island, and Westport and Fall River, Massachusetts. There are several villages associated with Tiverton and Little Compton: Stone Bridge, Four Corners, Adamsville, Bridgeport, Westport Point, Warren's Point and S'connet Point.

Tiverton and Little Compton, Rhode Island, are located east of Mount Hope Bay, composed primary of rock corresponding with the eastern half of Bristol Neck, while the upper end of Rhode Island, thrust between them, is of transition gray wacke. Mount Hope is composed of granite on its western side and white quartz on its eastern. Mount Hope Bay makes a southerly line from Fall River through Tiverton and Little Compton to the extreme point of Sakonnet, which forms the southeastern extremity of the Sakonnet River.[1]

PREFACE

In 1746, when Tiverton along with Little Compton, Bristol, Warren and Cumberland were declared the eastern boundary of Rhode Island by enforcement of royal decree, about 122 square miles were incorporated within the jurisdiction of the colony of Rhode Island and Providence Plantations.

Because of the towns' physical separation from the greater part of the state (part of Newport County), bordered on the east by Massachusetts and on the west by the east passage of Mount Hope Bay, the towns are, in effect, islands.

The towns' locations, landforms, ponds and streams, vegetation and climate all played important parts in their historical development. These qualities continue to play a role in shaping residents' sense of place.

INTRODUCTION

TIVERTON

The home and hunting lands of the Pocasset tribe held little interest to the English of the Rhode Island and Plymouth colonies because of supposed difficulty of raising crops in the rocky and hilly soil and swampy lowland. Another reason was that the Pocasset Indians were perceived to not be the type likely to make desirable neighbors—therefore, the Pocasset country was not in the jurisdiction of Rhode Island but rather was the outlying territory of the Plymouth Colony.

The history of Tiverton may be regarded as beginning in 1629 when William Bradford and his associates in the Plymouth Colony obtained a charter that placed the boundary of the colony at the Narragansett River. The "Narragansett River" referred to in the charter is the Sakonnet.[2] The Plymouth Colony held its jurisdiction over the territory for 116 years.

The new town received the name Tiverton after the town of Tiverton, England. Tiverton was annexed to Rhode Island in 1746, and this date is generally listed as the date of incorporation. In 1757, the population of the town included 842 English, 99 blacks and 99 Indians, totaling 1,040.

On the southeastern end of Mount Hope Bay, where the channel of the Sakonnet River enters it, the quiet town of Tiverton reposes. Yet it is not inert, for during the nineteenth century, its own little fleet of seining vessels carried on a very respectable trade, for which its geographic location is admirably adapted.

Every August during those days, Tiverton hosted a celebration, including speeches, aerial fireworks, a parade and much music designed to keep alive the memory of the day of the town's founding. A town that displays such honest and contented pride in its existence is certainly worth a visit; in earlier times, many who visited stayed in this delightful place.

Tiverton is doubly interesting because of its geographical position and its history. Originally known by the Native American name of Pocasset, it is celebrated as the scene of the great peasefield fight in King Philip's War. During the British occupancy of Newport, the American army was garrisoned in Tiverton. The so-called Battle of Tiverton Heights occurred on August 29, 1778. When the Americans' French allies finally took possession of Newport, the Tiverton barracks were assigned to them for hospital purposes, as was Point Pleasant Farm in Bristol.

Among the notable men whose names are associated with Tiverton's history is that of Joseph Wanton, one of the most successful shipbuilders in the colony. Many famous merchantmen and infamous privateers launched from Wanton's yard. A Quaker, Wanton is particularly remembered for his hospitality but also for his patriotic zeal and his interest in public affairs. Local tales abound of his open-door policy for any person who came hungry or destitute to his home.

Walton and his wife were speakers of the Society of Friends; his religious oratory at Quaker meetings is recalled as "extraordinary." He was the eldest son of Edward Wanton Sr., who followed and enlarged his father's shipbuilding business. Two of his brothers were governors of the colony, and in time, his son, Gideon, assumed the same esteemed office. His nephew and namesake, Joseph Wanton II, was the last Tory governor of the Rhode Island Colony. When America's Independence was won, the State of Rhode Island confiscated his lands.

Little Compton

English colonists knew little of the history of the Sakonnet lands before its settlement in the seventeenth century. The Sakonnets, one of the subtribes of the Wampanoag nation, occupied an area that included present-day Little Compton. Second- and third-generation English colonists, including from Plymouth Plantation, Massachusetts Bay and Rhode Island, were constantly seeking expansion, thus diminishing Indian lands.

The acquisition of land in Sakonnet did not occur quickly or easily. In 1666, a group of petitioners successfully appealed to the Massachusetts General Court to allow the group to purchase land at Sakonnet. Awashonks, the female sachem of the Sakonnets, declined to negotiate the sale of the tribe's land. However, in the early 1670s, Awashonks began to show an inclination to negotiate with the English. Her justification of solicitation for English protection came on the heels of theft of arms by one of her tribe for Wampanoag sachem Metacomet (King Philip). Evidently, not all members of her tribe supported her treaty with the English. The transfer of Sakonnet land from the Indians to the English caused a rift among tribe members, thus adding fuel to the eventual eruption of America's first shedding of native and colonial blood in all-out war.

The first settlement in the area was made in 1674 by Captain Benjamin Church, the vanquisher of Metacomet. Little Compton, located in the southeast corner of Rhode Island, is slightly more than twenty-three square miles, which composes just over 2 percent of the state's land area. The long, three-mile-wide town juts into the Atlantic Ocean at S'connet Point, at the southwest mouth of the east passage of the Sakonnet River. More than half of Little Compton's border is defined by seashore. However, the absence of a deep natural harbor discouraged intense maritime development.

This town, as well as Tiverton to the north, is part of the mainland, politically separated from the state of Massachusetts, which the town was a part of until 1747. Little Compton's isolation has been a key reinforcing factor in the town's development throughout its history.

Glacial activity during the most recent ice age formed the town's topography. The ice sheet deposited soil and boulders, shaping the land into one of softly rising and falling hills. Today, the land rises gently from the water and rolls in hills, shallow valleys and marshes. Woodlands fill slightly less than half of the town's land. Farming occupies 19 percent of the land, and grazing grasses fill most of the uncultivated land. Black, red and white oak and hickory predominate, with scattered stands of hemlock and white pine.

Like other seaside towns in southern New England, Little Compton's climate is relatively moderate, warmed in winter by the Gulf Stream current of the Atlantic Ocean and cooled in summer by temperate sea breezes. Rainfall averages between forty and forty-five inches per year. These conditions have long encouraged agriculture.

TIVERTON

A Historical Prospective

*Tiverton originally belonged to Massachusetts Bay Colony but in 1747,
by royal decree it became part of Rhode Island Colony. At Fort Barton
on Tiverton Heights is a revolutionary earthwork erected to command the
water during the British occupation of Newport on Aquidneck Island. It
was from Tiverton that Captain William Barton set out on his historic
expedition that resulted in the capture of the nightshirt clad British General
Richard Prescott. At Tiverton is the home of Captain Robert Gray,
commander of the first American vessel to enter the mouth of the Columbia
River in 1792 and the first to carry the flag of the United States around
the globe.*

—anonymous, 1936, scrap clipping

Tiverton is one of five towns of Rhode Island that formerly belonged
to Massachusetts. The indigenous name of Pocasset is the territory on
both sides of the Sakonnet River; a portion of the territory formed a part
of the first settlement known as the Pocasset Purchase, which occurred in
1680. The southern portion of the town was known, at that time, by the
name of Puncatust.

In 1680, Plymouth colonists purchased this region from the natives and then
sold it to Edward Gray and seven other Englishmen for the sum of £1,200.
Tiverton, like its southern neighbor Sakonnet (Little Compton), was governed
by the female sachem Weetamoe,[3] queen of the Pocasset tribe.

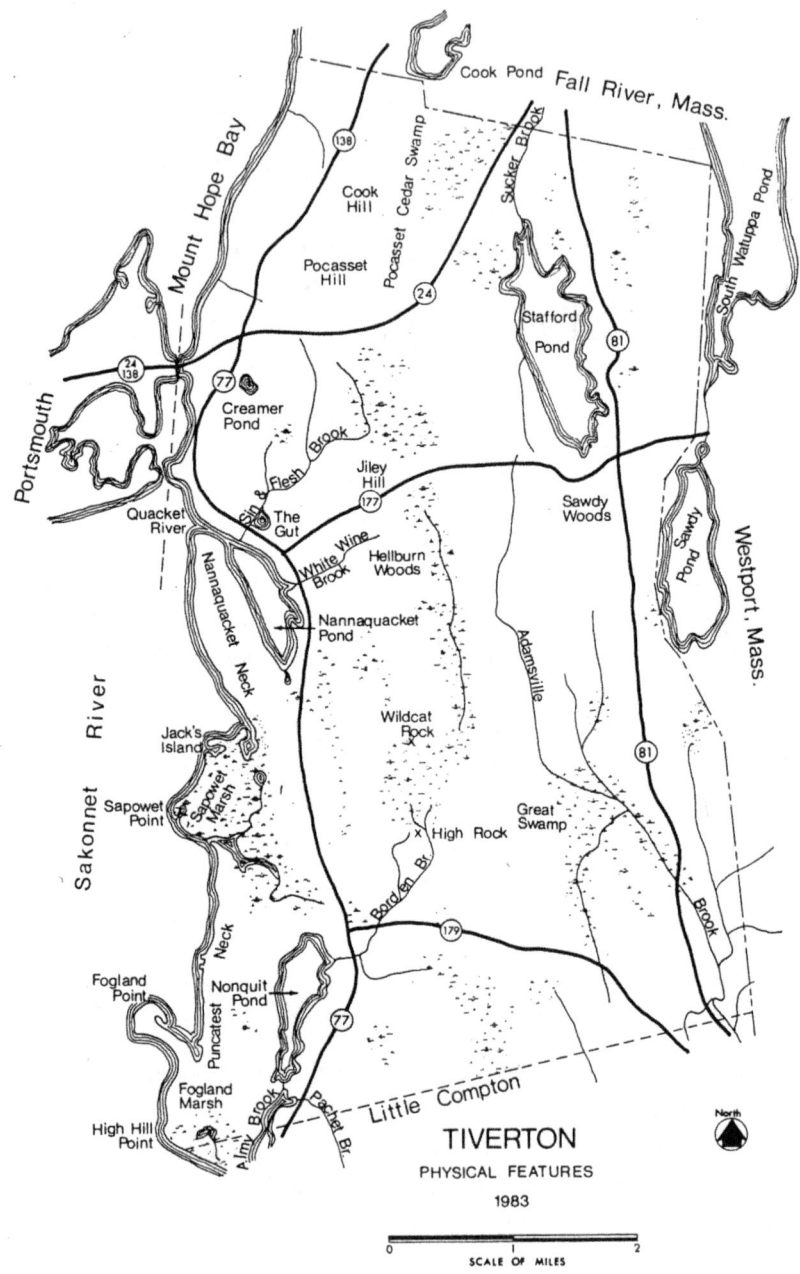

Cook Pond

Fall River, Mass.

138

Sucker Brook

Cook Hill

Pocasset Cedar Swamp

Pocasset Hill

24

Stafford Pond

81

South Waluppa Pond

Mount Hope Bay

Portsmouth

24
138

77

Creamer Pond

Flesh Brook

Jiley Hill

177

Sawdy Woods

Sandy Pond

Westport, Mass.

Quacket River

The Gut

White Wine Brook

Hellburn Woods

Nannaquacket Pond

Nannaquacket Neck

Adamsville

Sakonnet River

Jack's Island

Wildcat Rock
X

Sapowet Point

Sapowet Marsh

81

High Rock
X

Great Swamp

Borden Br.

Brook

Fogland Point

Nonquit Pond

Puncatest Neck

179

Fogland Marsh

77

High Hill Point

Almy Brook

Pachet Br.

Little Compton

TIVERTON

PHYSICAL FEATURES

1983

North

0   1   2

SCALE OF MILES

Topographic map of Tiverton, drawn in 1983.

Unlike the female sachem Awashonks of Sakonnet, Weetamoe joined with King Philip against the English. She proved to be one of Philip's most faithful and efficient supporters. When the number of her fighting men was reduced from three hundred to only twenty-six, they fled to the security of a swamp in Swansea. Endeavoring to escape by night by crossing Mount Hope Bay on a raft, Weetamoe drowned, preferring death to capture by the whites.

SETTLEMENT

Tiverton was incorporated as a township in 1694, and Rhode Island annexed it in 1746. A portion of the town was set off and given to Fall River in 1862 at the time of the final settlement of the disputed boundary between Massachusetts and Rhode Island. During the War of Independence, a large camp of American solders occupied Tiverton Heights.

The easternmost part of Rhode Island consists of this narrow strip of land contained between the present Massachusetts line on the east and the waterways of the Sakonnet River and Mount Hope Bay on the west. Before the Mount Hope Bridge and the Stone Bridge, the only access was by land, passing through a considerable part of Massachusetts and the city of Fall River.

In total, the combined size of Tiverton and Little Compton is about ten miles long and nearly three and a half miles wide; Tiverton's principal settlements are North Tiverton, Tiverton and Tiverton Four Corners.

A panoramic view of the Tiverton Stone Bridge shoreline across the Sakonnet River from Portsmouth, 1997.

The Old Stone Bridge with its steel and iron draw.

Tiverton is chiefly an agricultural town, though during the late 1800s and the first decade of the twentieth century, a lucrative fishing and menhaden oil processing business was one of the primary industrial pursuits. Cotton and woolen mills were established as early as 1827.

The Stone Bridge from Tiverton to Aquidneck Island's Hummocks was Tiverton's principal access to Portsmouth and Newport and, later, to Greater Rhode Island after construction of the Mount Hope Bridge in 1927.

EARLY PROMINENT FAMILY NAMES

Many of Tiverton's early settlers, who engaged in fishing, whaling and farming, became associated with certain localities. We can associate the Almy family with Puncatest Neck, the Cook and Gray families with the southwest part of town, the Crandalls with Crandallville and the Humphrey family with Nannaquaket Neck. Other prominent family groups included the Hamblys, Hicks, Manchesters and Kings, though these were more widespread.

Several families achieved great prominence, their fame and reputation spreading beyond the town's borders. Dr. William Whitridge, who settled in Tiverton in 1770, became a well-known and respected physician. Three of his sons became doctors as well, and another son became a successful businessman. Born and raised in Tiverton, they all eventually established their personal residences in other locations.

Dr. Whitridge's daughter, Mary, married Samuel West II, also a successful physician and the father of Dr. Samuel West III. The third Samuel West, a graduate of Harvard Medical School, married Mary Durfee of Nannaquaket Neck. Her father, Job, served in the United States Congress. Job and his son, Thomas, served as chief justices of the Rhode Island Supreme Court. All were well-known public speakers, essayists and poets.

INDUSTRY AND COMMERCE

Farming and secondary occupations such as blacksmithing, tavern keeping, ferrying, shipbuilding, whaling, trading and operating small sawmills and gristmills prevailed through the eighteenth century.

The view from Tiverton Heights showing pogy boats in the Sakonnet River, with Portsmouth in the background. The outcropping of granite in the middle background is the Portsmouth Hummocks.

A pair of pogy boats chugs along the Sakonnet River, as seen from the Hummocks. In the background is the shoreline at Tiverton Heights, circa 1919.

Tiverton remained an agricultural town during the nineteenth century. Other enterprises—including milling, textile manufacturing, whaling, coasting[4] and commercial fishing—came, declined and eventually disappeared. Regional fishermen played premier roles in the menhaden fish industry during the course of about forty years from 1870 to 1910.

In the latter part of the 1890s, wind was a source of power; there were several windmills in rural areas along the shore. Small water-powered sawmills, gristmills and textile mills were operated in 1895. Ice harvesting developed in the latter part of the century, and several icehouses were built on the shore of the small pond south of Nannaquaket Pond, along Mill Pond at Tiverton Four Corners, beside Sin and Flesh Brook and on the northwest shore of Stafford Pond. In about 1874, on the Borden Brook at Main Road, William Pitt Bateman purchased the mill site and built a new gristmill, a store and a wheelwright shop. Pittsville was the name of the place until about 1866. Water-powered sawmills and gristmills continued operations, serving the surrounding farms well into the nineteenth century.

Although Tiverton was not a major textile manufacturing center, three water-powered textile mills sprung up during the first half of the nineteenth century. Two of the sites had preexisting sawmills and gristmills. Along Sucker Brook, just below Stafford Pond, George Durfee and Asa Coggeshall purchased a sawmill and gristmill site in about 1828 and built a stone cotton factory, a stone woolen factory, several houses and a general store. There were never more than a few buildings in this small community known as Eagleville. In 1850, the fittingly named Eagle Mill employed three men and five women for the manufacturing of carpet warps. Destroyed by fire in 1861, the woolen mill was never rebuilt.

In 1844, Sylvanus Nickerson built his thread mill located near a sawmill and gristmill site along Sin and Flesh Brook. This mill changed hands many times before being destroyed by fire in 1864. In the extreme southeastern corner of town, Christopher Brownell built his Adamsville Carding Mill in 1850. The Adamsville mill employed two men and two women, but this factory closed down well before the turn of the century.

Industry remained small scale for most of the town in the late nineteenth century. Major developments were restricted to the northern fringe of Tiverton, adjacent to Fall River. In the 1890s, two large cotton mills were built in the extreme northern part of town. The mills were unrelated to the other Tiverton mills but were part of the Fall River system and dominated by Fall River manufacturers. In 1872, the Shove Mills Stock Company was incorporated in Massachusetts, and the company built a mill just within the Fall River, Massachusetts state line.

In 1880, the Shove Company built a second mill in Tiverton, a three-story granite structure housing 22,208 spindles and 125 employees who did the spinning and carding for the earlier mill. In 1881–82, the Bourne Company built a larger, four-story granite mill with an imposing, mansard-roofed central tower. In 1888, the Bourne Mill kept 500 employees busy running 1,080 looms and 43,008 spindles, making all kinds of textile goods.

FERRIES AND SOUND STEAMERS

During the 1700s and 1800s, when roads were poor and overland travel was difficult, much cargo and some travelers preferred the water route. Small sailing vessels with shallow drafts, the so-called coasters, negotiated the shallow and restrictive waters of Narragansett Bay and the Sakonnet River. Tiverton captain Peleg Cory ran a trading sloop from his wharf at Puncatest Neck to Providence, carrying goods and supplies for Tiverton Four Corners merchants. Later, Peleg's son, Thomas, sailed a sloop for more than twenty years. Still later, Benjamin Wilcox sailed a packet to Providence, and Holder N. Wilcox operated a freight and passenger boat, the *Temperance*.

The ferry *West Side* approaches its temporary slip and dock in this O.E. Dubois photograph dated June 6, 1907. The *West Side* was pressed into service during one of the numerous repairs to the Stone Bridge.

The Stone Bridge crosses the Sakonnet River at its most narrow point, circa 1912.

Tiverton has enjoyed a lasting and important association with Aquidneck Island. The reason for this association is twofold: Aquidneck Island is the closest established Rhode Island community to Tiverton, and the establishment of a ferry at the narrows between the Sakonnet River and Mount Hope Bay created the safest place and narrowest passage between Aquidneck and the mainland.

The history of the Tiverton-Aquidneck ferry service is long, complex and interesting. The first ferry here, and perhaps the first authorized service in Rhode Island, was licensed to Thomas Gorton in 1640. From 1694 until well into the nineteenth century, both the ferry and the immediate area on the Tiverton side were known as Howland's Ferry. Another ferry, often referred to as the "northernmost" ferry, was established in 1680. Thomas Durfee of Portsmouth was most likely the first proprietor of this ferry, which ran from the Hummocks to Humphrey's Wharf in Tiverton. Durfee's Ferry was also known as the Pocasset Ferry and Anthony's Ferry.

The northern ferry continued operations into the late eighteenth century. Howland's Ferry remained in service longer, likely continuing service after construction of the Stone Bridge in 1794–95 (the bridge was closed from 1796 to 1810).

In 1707, Captain Thomas Townsend petitioned to establish a ferry at Fogland Point that would link the Dartmouth Road with Aquidneck Island, accessing Newport. Townsend's stepson, Job Almy, was authorized to run the ferry in 1715. Almy gave bond to provide a good boat with sails and oars. Almy's Ferry is mentioned in legislative acts of 1747, 1752 and 1767 that fixed rates of ferriage. The Fogland Point Ferry provided service until the beginning of hostilities between the Americans and British and until the British initiated a blockade interrupting the run.

The Dartmouth Road grew in importance because of the Fogland Point Ferry. In 1710, a committee from Puncatest and Sakonnet laid out thirty building sites—the nucleus of the village of Tiverton Four Corners. The mill and the village were called Nomcot, later Nonquit, and the same can be said of the name of the nearby pond.

In about 1863, Isaac White purchased Cory's Wharf at Puncatest Neck, the name being changed to White's Wharf. In 1870, Alexander Pierce built a new wharf a short distance north of White's. Several steamers, which provided service for thirty years between S'connet Point and Providence, used Pierce's Wharf. The steamer service made daily or twice daily runs in summer, less frequently in other seasons.

Captain Horatio N. Wilcox pioneered the steamboat runs with *Dolphin*, his little steamer. Wilcox's service began in 1886; he served farmers, fishermen and tradesmen in moving their goods along the Sakonnet.

In 1887, Tiverton resident Captain Julius A. Pettey purchased the steamer *Queen City*, beginning runs in competition with Wilcox. Pettey founded the Sakonnet Transportation Company, which in 1893 added the *Awashonks* steamer to its little fleet. Pettey encouraged day-trippers to use his steamers by building a dining pavilion at S'connet Point.

MARITIME ACTIVITIES

The sea provided alternative or supplementary occupations for Tiverton men, who undoubtedly fished and engaged in the coastal trade in addition to operating ferries. The sea and the bay were important sources of fish for food, oil and fertilizers, products of importance to Tiverton's late nineteenth-century economy. The menhaden is an abundant fish—though some say an inedible one. Native Americans called the fish *munnawhatteaug*, which is thought to translate to "fish that fertilizes."

The menhaden fishing industry started in about 1850 when a Maine woman bottled some "fish water" and sent it to an oil merchant in Boston.

The Tiverton approach to the Old Stone Bridge, circa 1906. Howland's Ferry operated here until about 1794. In 1795, a toll bridge was built and operated by the Rhode Island Bridge Company. The Sakonnet River's strong current and several severe storms destroyed the bridge a number of times, but it was always rebuilt with improved technology.

Evidently, the merchant's estimate of the value of the oil was so encouraging that within one year, one hundred barrels of menhaden oil had been sent to Boston. By 1870, the menhaden oil industry exceeded the total of whale, seal and codfish oil made in the United States.

Rhode Island's involvement in the menhaden industry began when Joseph Church settled in Tiverton in 1838 and became a commercial fisherman. In 1870, Church and his seven sons incorporated as Joseph Church and Sons for the manufacture of menhaden oil, guano and fertilizer. The company flourished into the twentieth century with a processing plant, four large wharves, outbuildings, drying and storage sheds and a drying field, all situated on twenty acres at Common Fence Point in Portsmouth.

Several other entrepreneurs also profited in the menhaden industry. Isaac White built a wharf at Pukatest and a fish and oil factory nearby. In 1874, the firm of William J. Brightman and Company organized to engage in the production of fish oil and fertilizer. A common complaint during the heyday of the menhaden processing was the foul odor wafting on the air, to which the common reply of factory owners was: "Smells like money to me."

In 1773, Gideon Almy's sloop, the *Sally*, was seized by French privateers and condemned with a cargo of whale oil while on a whaling voyage to the West Indies. This is one of the earliest records of a Tiverton-owned whaling ship and of Tiverton's association with the sea, which reached its zenith in the nineteenth century. In the latter part of the 1700s, two Tiverton men were engaged in the fur trade and working in the Pacific Northwest. Cornelius Soule, a fur trapper, was also engaged in the China trade; his partner, Captain Robert Gray, commander of the trading ship *Columbia*, was the first American to sail the Columbia River, thus helping establish the United States' claim to the Oregon Territory. The homes of both men still stand along Main Road at and near Tiverton Four Corners.

WHALING

While most Tiverton folks worked the land, a considerable number turned their attention seaward to engage in catching whales and processing their oil, a most lucrative business in the nineteenth century.

Originally a land-based enterprise in the waters of Nantucket, the industry spread to southeastern Massachusetts and Rhode Island. The earliest record of whaling in Rhode Island is 1733, when the first fully equipped whaleman arrived at Newport. The broadside *Starbuck* records in 1876 that the whale fishery was long carried on in a small way within the Rhode Island Colony; whales were frequently taken by boats in Narragansett Bay. Bristol and Warren, Rhode Island, became thriving whaling ports beginning in the mid-eighteenth century. Tiverton's orientation was toward the east, to nearby Westport, Fairhaven and New Bedford, Massachusetts. Whaling voyages were made from nearby Westport from 1775. During the industry's peak, Westport vessels engaged in whale hunting, at any one time numbering from twenty to thirty. The greatest number of Tiverton's whalemen sailed aboard the *Industry* and the *Almy*.

New Bedford was the center of the whaling industry for the entire East Coast between 1835 and 1859, the golden age of whaling. By the end of the mid-nineteenth century, 329 vessels and about twelve thousand seamen had sailed out of New Bedford searching for what at the time seemed to be an inexhaustible resource. The whaling industry brought wealth to the whaling ports until about 1876, when kerosene came into common use, gradually replacing whale oil for lamps and heating. However, whalers continued sailing from New Bedford with Tiverton seamen until the early twentieth century.

Although Tiverton was not a whaling port, the town's association and identity with this industry is strong. Information compiled at the New Bedford Library and the Providence Public Library confirms that between 1808 and 1898, Tiverton men identified as seamen made 391 voyages aboard whaling ships. Further, the major years of activity in the shipboard industry for Tiverton whalemen is from about 1820 to about 1875.

Whaling voyage records from 1731 to 1925 list eighteen Tiverton whaling captains who made forty-three voyages. Five whaling captains lived on Crandall Road. Captain Allen Hart went to sea in 1823 at age sixteen and continued as a whaleman for twenty-eight years, and Amasa Simmons sailed for twenty years, also beginning at age sixteen. Many of the whale hunts were of relatively short duration, less than a year; however, some men were gone from home on three- to four-year voyages. Several Tiverton whalers survived shipwrecks, while others, including Andrew Cory's two brothers, were lost at sea.

Although Tiverton was not a major whaling port, many Tiverton-ported ships sailed as part of the Rhode Island whaling fleet. The town's association and identity with the sea is strong.

TIVERTON YACHT CLUB

After the destruction of the Fall River Yacht Club in the 1938 hurricane, former members were largely responsible for founding the Tiverton Yacht Club in 1945. By the fall of 1946, the club's register listed more than five hundred members. The *Providence Journal* made the following report on the growth of the club:

> *Tiverton, long noted for the fishing activity carried on along its waterfront, is developing a new complex for its shores with the growth of the Tiverton Yacht Club. The opening of the club and the return of many young sailing enthusiasts from the service* [World War II] *are credited with a startling increase in the number of pleasure boats that anchor off the town. Sailing boats outnumber power by about three to one in the club fleet.*

In 1947, Stewart Grinnell became the club's first commodore, and with other flag officers, they ran the club's affairs. Yachting and social activities developed side by side, and on May 30, 1947, three hundred members attended a buffet supper. Later that year, the Candy Boat Association was formed. Racing in the basin had already begun in earnest, and ashore there were clambakes, supper dances, card parties and much more. Junior activities, besides sailing, included dances, swims, mystery rides and beach parties.

At first, the club leased the second floor of a building on a dock in the Stone Bridge area, after the owner agreed to renovate the rooms to the club's specifications.

In September 1955, the club announced plans to buy the former Holden estate on Riverside Drive for use as a year-round facility, complete with tennis courts, a bathing beach and a wharf. When the purchase went through, the club took occupancy of the beautiful three-story building with a wide wraparound veranda, located near the waterfront and the club's dock. Unfortunately, the building was destroyed by a fire in 2003.

History of the Tiverton Yacht Club

The following was written by Richard Toolin in June 2012.

The 1938 hurricane swept away the Fall River Yacht Club located on Riverside Drive in Tiverton, Rhode Island, immediately south of the current Tiverton Yacht Club and directly across the street from the John Moran homestead; and for several years this terminated formal boating activities in the Tiverton Basin.

Continued interest in yachting, especially Candy Class sailboat racing spurred a group of Tivertonians to launch a drive for a new yacht club in the fall of 1945. Several informal meetings were held in the home of Carlton Grinnell and the first organizational meeting was held at the home of Stewart Grinnell, who became the club's first secretary.

At this organizational meeting, the Tiverton Yacht Club, Inc. (TYC) was formed and the following officers were elected: president, George U. Parks; vice-president, Edgar J. Cyr; secretary and chairman of publicity, Stewart Grinnell; treasurer, Carlton Grinnell; board of directors, Carleton Grinnell, chairman; Mr. Cyr, Mr. Parks, Norman Ross, Melvin Sanford, Commander Clarence E. Wood, Milton Shovelton, Howard Gibbs and Earle Hathaway.

It was decided to lease the second floor of the building on the dock at the foot of Middle Ave. [now Standish Boatyard], whose new owners, Henry Walsh, his son, Harry and son-in law James Mataronas, had agreed to install a soda bar, cover the walls with knotty pine, lay a hardwood floor in the clubroom, construct a large porch on the second floor waterside and build a bridge directly from the street side second floor to the Main Road sidewalk for easy access. Additionally, a 20-foot addition was built on the building south end, giving the TYC a 60 x 30 foot area. The south water frontage of the wharf was to be for the exclusive use of the members of the new club. Point of interest, the facility had just been purchased by Mr. Walsh's group from Francis Manchester.

A successful membership drive in the spring of 1946 ensured a healthy future for the new TYC when it held its first annual meeting at Whitridge Hall, Lawton Avenue in Tiverton's Stone Bridge area, on April 11. At this meeting, new by-laws were accepted and the names of Irving D. Humphrey, Jr. and Walsh Leach were added to the board of directors. The new officers elected were: president, George Parks; vice-president, Melvin Sanford; treasurer, Carleton Grinnell; and secretary, Jean Ann Grinnell.

The first meeting of the TYC board of directors was held on May 3 when the first flag officers of the new club were elected. They were: Commodore, Stewart Grinnell; Vice-Commodore, Gilbert Van Blarcom; Rear-Commodore, L. Sanford Chace Jr.; Fleet Surgeon, Dr. Owen Eagan; Measurer, T. Elton Wood; Assistant Measurer, Milton Shovelton.

The 1946 season proved to be a busy one for the new officers who organized the first formal racing schedule, a series of social events, and provided all sorts of new equipment for the club. It was this group of enthusiastic yachtsmen who set the pattern for all subsequent activities for several happy and successful years.

During this period of expansion, the Tiverton Candy Boat Fleet [the primary sailboat racing class of the Tiverton Yacht Club] increased in size to a registration of 42 boats, and the powerboat fleet numbered 26, with the total membership of 206 yacht club individuals.

Toward the end of the 1947 season, while Carleton Grinnell was president and Robert T. Richards commodore, several important changes were made in the by-laws. It was voted to abolish the system of dual officers and to instruct the running of the club to the flag officers and board of directors. The board was to consist of fifteen members, five to be elected per year for a three-year term. Space will not permit the listing of all the loyal members who have done so much to ensure the success of the Tiverton Yacht Club since its incorporation.

Riverside Drive

As the club continued to grow and as its activities became more diversified, it became apparent that the physical equipment was no longer adequate. Interest increased for quarters that are more suitable and in November 1955, a committee was appointed to find a new site. The purchase of the building and grounds at 54 Riverside Drive, the old "Faucett House," from TYC member Ken Brown, enabled the Club to auspiciously open the 1956 season with the added facilities of a bathing beach, senior and junior quarters, a separate galley and new clubhouse furnishings, a new wharf, outdoor barbeque, horseshoe and shuffleboard courts as well as additional furnishings were added in the following years.

At the close of the 1958 season TYC family membership had increased to 152 with well over 300 juniors and 27 single adult members. With a total membership in excess of 600 and physical facilities considered among the finest in the Narragansett Bay area, with one of the most active social and racing calendars on the whole east coast, the Club has certainly come a long way since 1945.

In 1970, the Club's leadership decided to undertake enclosing the clubhouse's front porch and building a second floor deck over the old front porch. Alvin Litchfield performed construction, furnishing donated by Ralph Cutillo of Stone Bridge Inn and the new enclosed front porch was tiled by Phil Drapeau of Allied Floor Covering. These tasks resulted in an expanded second floor senior area and a larger gathering and dining area on the main floor.

In the early 1970s, the Candy class participation was beginning to diminish because of deteriorating wooden boat conditions and a desire to introduce a one-design fiberglass racing class. The Club's very active racing group met and coordinated the purchase of over 30 Sunfish; revitalizing the junior and senior weekly racing programs. Very active Sunfish racing was observed at the TYC for the next 20 years. In 1978, the TYC undertook renovation of its beach locker facility, expanding the number of lockers to about 38.

In 1987 the Club undertook two major transformations: the simple "T" dock became a small "3 fingered" marina with slip accommodations for a limited number of members and a large in-ground swimming pool was installed adjacent to the club house on the property's south yard. The swimming pool, with shallow and deep ends, provided both member enjoyment and family swimming lesson capability. The beachfront continues to be available for those members who prefer sunbathing by the river or swimming in the salt water. Unfortunately, the addition of the marina resulted in the loss of our long enjoyed raft that was configured with both low and high diving boards, and a slide.

In June 2003, the yacht club was destroyed by fire. Fortunately, no one was injured, as the clubhouse had not yet opened for the season. Unfortunately, all of the yacht club records, trophies and memorials were destroyed. The fire was attributed to an electrical problem. Since the fire, the Board of Directors are working tirelessly to obtain all the necessary permits to allow the club to rebuild. Unfortunately, our immediate neighbors have relentlessly challenged the permits. At this writing [June 2012], the club has yet to rebuild and the matter is before the RI State Supreme Court.

Since the fire, the TYC continues its summer season operations using a tent as a temporary facility and a bathroom trailer. The swimming programs and sail training programs continue with full enrollment. The cruising class weekly races continue with good attendance. Family and adult functions are still scheduled and are actively attended throughout the summer season. In spite of the difficulties with rebuilding the clubhouse, the TYC has continued as an active junior and senior sailboat-racing club, with vigorous sail training and swimming programs. Membership totals have fluctuated over the years but continue to be strong in the 150–160 family range. The club is proud to be one of the few in the area providing an excellent social and yachting opportunity for those who desire the convenience of a family oriented and family friendly experience.

MODERN TIMES

The coming of the railroad was instrumental in developing the town's recreational potential at Tiverton Heights and along the shore below. Other sections, including Nannaquaket Neck[5] and Puncatest Neck, were choice locations for large country estates established by wealthy southerners seeking to escape metropolitan cities' sultry summer heat.

In the twentieth century, the automobile put the entire town within easy reach of nearby urban centers. After World War II, the once rural area became a residential suburb of Fall River. Farming, fishing and recreation became minor activities in the mid-twentieth century compared to their importance in the previous century. Today, the town is a multifaceted community set within an essentially urban-suburban context.

The cotton mills are no longer active, the whaling sperm oil industry is just a memory, the giant overnight steamers and commuter ferries are long gone and only a small number of the population is engaged in farming and fishing. However, the lives and activities of Tiverton's former residents have left important legacies: Native American sites, seventeenth- and eighteenth-century military and battle sites, villages, farms, houses, mill sites, schools, churches, wharves and bridges—all of which constitute the important components of Tiverton's heritage.

Architectural and Historical Landmarks

Early Dwellings

A nearly landlocked inlet named Nannaquaket Pond is located just south of Tiverton Center. Most of the town's oldest dwellings are along this old waterfront road.

The residence thought to be the oldest remaining house in the region is seen at the edge of the garden in the rear of the David Durfee House, on the eastern side of this road, a little to the south of Nannaquaket Pond. A long, low, narrow, one-story stone masonry building—with most of its interior work having been removed decades earlier—was used as a wood storage shed for a considerable time. Originally, it had only two rooms, with separating partitions at the right of the center doorway, as viewed from the eastern garden side. While the exact date of construction of this building is unknown, it undoubtedly belongs to the early decades of the 1700s.

The Durfee House, built in 1768, remains especially well maintained. Successive owners have treated this dwelling lovingly. The doorway is one of several of very similar types seen in this region; it is distinctive because of its extreme height and narrow proportions.

The example of a doorway that appears on another Durfee homestead, standing a little farther to the north, displays some extremely delicate details more unusual and locally characteristic than the earlier example on the

Quahog harvesters working in Nannaquaket Pond; a house called Nannaquaket is in the background, circa 1920.

David Durfee House. This house is a later development of the same type, built by perhaps the next or following generation of the same family.

Known locally as the Nathaniel Briggs House, this old residence is one of the most interesting in the region. Local authority places its construction before 1777. As it now stands, the portion facing south on the old garden is the oldest part, the northern end having been built to replace the earlier kitchen and servants' quarters that were in an extreme state of disrepair through long neglect. In the process of this renovation, the original staircase was lost, including the large and spacious old kitchen, planned for the period when slaves were the family retainers.

Tory lieutenant governor Oliver once owned the property. During the heat of the struggle for independence, he fled to England, and the state confiscated the place. It is now one of the few remaining old manor houses of the region, reflecting in New England something of the vanished life and atmosphere of the old plantations along the southern Atlantic coast.

Whitridge Hall, located on Lawton Avenue, is a two-story structure with a large, square tower at the left side of the front and a one-story section at the rear built in 1876. Thomas Whitridge offered the first contribution toward construction of the building, and with donations from others, a combined chapel and hall was built. The Whitridge Hall Association managed the property until the Tiverton Historical Society emerged.

Left: The Nathaniel Briggs House as seen from the garden, circa 1920.

Below: The Nathaniel Briggs–Manchester–Beattle House (pre-1777), 66 Indian Point Road, January 1997.

Doorway of the John Cooke House, circa 1920. Caleb Cory built the structure in 1775.

The John Cooke House, built sometime before 1775. Notice the heavy hewn plank widow caps on this building.

The Unitarian Chapel, called Bowen Memorial, was opened in June 1876. Services ended shortly after 1900. Among those conducting services were Reverend Edward Everett Hale and Julia Ward Howe.[6] The building also contained a library and a reading room, and the Episcopalians held social events in the hall before the Episcopal church was built. In the 1950s, a summer theater troupe used the Whitridge Hall, and in the 1960s, it was used as a dance hall. When public use of the building ceased, it was converted to an apartment house.

At Tiverton Center, there is a weathered old house, supposedly built in 1775 by local carpenter Caleb Cory for John Cooke. The moldings and clapboards on the west front, which were exposed to three centuries of weather without surface protection, are worn almost to wafer thinness at some places. The heavy hewn plank window caps on this building are also worthy of note for their unusually sturdy type.

Another old house in North Tiverton is known as the Thomas Osborn Homestead. The date of construction is thought to be prior to 1766 because Osborn is known to have lived there between 1766 and 1833.

The ornate doors and casings of the Nathaniel Briggs House. The south entry is at left and the side doorway at right.

There are many other smaller and less important types of dwellings scattered all about Tiverton, one of which is the old John Gray House, one of the oldest, dating from about 1700. First used as a tavern, it is one of the earliest structures in the region, and the home of the seven Church brothers. Set at its unusual site, on the border of a little fishing inlet, the grace and charm of its neat proportions and spacious gambrel roof ends are fully visible and appreciated.

There are a number of so-called Cape Cod cottage types along this shoreline, such as the James Otis Hamby Cottage and many others.

THE NANNAQUAKET BRIDGE

Before the 1938 hurricane, a wooden bridge crossed the Quacket River to Nannaquaket Pond beyond. In an act dated May 1875, the Rhode Island General Assembly authorized George W. Humphrey and others to erect a bridge across the strait leading into Nannaquaket Pond, providing, however, "that the said bridge shall be constructed at a place and upon a plan to be approved by the town council."

Charles E. Davis of Woods Hole won the contract for construction, signed July 5, 1883. Work began in early August and finished about one month later. The contracted cost of construction was $2,208, and the last two feet at the top of the structure were to be built by the owners, who evidently figured that they could build this part cheaper using their own labor.

Davis agreed to pay for the rocks and stone delivered to the construction site by the owners. In the final settlement, Davis allowed for 714 tons at forty cents per ton. Furnishing the stone required a great deal of work by men and oxen and, incidentally, resulted in the clearing of the fields and pastures of Nannaquaket.

The 1938 hurricane destroyed the stone- and rubble-filled causeway. Local stonemasons and laborers engaged to rebuild the 1883 bridge and were compensated at the rate of $0.15 per hour. Albert and Thomas Gray received the sum of $420.00 for use of the south end of their wharf on the east side of the river.

STONE BRIDGE AND
STONE BRIDGE INN

The historic Stone Bridge District is a loosely defined, unincorporated settlement sited in a relatively narrow area between Tiverton and Portsmouth and a rugged hill section to the east.

The first activity in Stone Bridge parallels the settlement of adjacent Portsmouth in 1638 and the establishment of a ferry in 1640. In 1674, John Simmons built a house and received a license to keep a tavern and accommodations for travelers, in addition to running the ferry. The Howland family acquired the ferry license in about 1700, running it until about 1776. Thus, the small settlement on the Tiverton side assumed the name Howland's Ferry. This designation remained throughout the eighteenth century and well into the following century.

OLD STONE BRIDGE

The opening of the Sakonnet River Bridge on September 25, 1956, brought to a close the 160-year battle between Rhode Islanders and the storm tides of the Sakonnet River.

The original Stone Bridge, built in 1794, linked Tiverton and Aquidneck Island during the next century. It was washed out twice, repaired and replaced with a new bridge in 1810. This bridge was lost in the Great Gale of 1815, and a new one took its place in 1817. The 1817 span lasted until

The Old Stone Bridge before the 1938 hurricane.

A new draw was installed on the Old Stone Bridge, and trolley tracks were laid in 1898. This photo was taken before 1938.

a storm carried it off in 1869; a new one was built the following year and another one in 1907. Somewhere along the line of succession, the spans picked up the name Old Stone Bridge. The small area of clustered buildings around the bridge became known as Stone Bridge Village.

The *Pease and Niles' Gazette* of 1819 relates merely that Stone Bridge, at the bridge at Howland's Ferry, is one of two villages in the town. *Hayward's Gazette* of 1839 also mentions Howland's Ferry at the Stone Bridge.

The 1907 bridge, built close to the water like its predecessors, continued to fall prey to every bad storm until it suffered serious damage in the hurricane of 1938 and Hurricane Carol in 1954. Soon, work began on another new bridge, closing the Old Stone's famous medieval-style draw for good and shutting off the Sakonnet River to navigation until the new bridge opened.

The need for a modern steel bridge was apparent long before this. The public learned of the plans for a four-lane fixed bridge over the river about three-quarters of a mile north of the Old Stone Bridge early in 1947. Peak traffic on the old span was reaching an average of seven thousand vehicles per day. By the end of construction in 1956, the Sakonnet River Bridge had become the state's most expensive public works project ever

The Portsmouth approach to the Stone Bridge. The span survived and saw service for 163 years except for temporary closings due to ship collisions and the hurricanes of 1938 and 1954.

An elevated view of the Sakonnet River railroad bridge from the Portsmouth Hummocks.

undertaken, with a final price tag of almost $9 million, almost twice the original estimate.

Much of the increase in cost was due to the unique geological structure of the Sakonnet River Basin, which is filled to a great depth with glacial deposits. Piles for the bridge were driven as deep as 378 feet below the water's surface, much deeper than any previous Rhode Island bridge required. Initial bridge surveys had not indicated the true depth of the bedrock.

The new span, a continuous through arch bridge with an overall length of 2,989 feet and a main reach over the channel at 375 feet, provides a clearance for navigation of 65 feet. The new span was distinctive in a number of ways; most important is the fact that it was toll free, drawing a good percentage of traffic in the direction of Fall River rather than over the Mount Hope toll bridge. Another feature was the lack of a high point at center span. Instead, the bridge rises continually from Portsmouth to the Tiverton Highlands.

As soon as the new bridge opened, the Old Stone Bridge was torn down, with only its stone approaches remaining in the river on each shore for the benefit of sport fishermen.

STONE BRIDGE INN

There has been an inn at the Stone Bridge area of Tiverton since even before there was a town, let alone a bridge.

July 7, 1640, is the date on the first license given to operate an inn. King Charles I of England's condition for granting approval of the original ferry service in the Pocasset area of the Massachusetts Bay was that accommodations for passengers be provided.

Built in 1790 by Captain Lawton, the Lawton House replaced the shanty inn of Howland's Ferry. Travelers seeking shelter as they journeyed from Newport to Boston frequented the Lawton House. Later, before its destruction by fire in 1847, the place became known as a resort.

Gardner Thomas erected a new inn in the same location. Thomas named his inn Stone Bridge Cottage and opened it for business on July 4, 1848. The "cottage" interior copied the rustic Adirondack style. Asa T. Lawton of Newport bought the inn in 1864, enlarging and improving it at the princely sum of $60,000. Lawton renamed the inn the Lawton House and opened it in 1865. The inn operated for two seasons before he sold it in 1867 to a company of thirty investors from Fall River that ran the inn until the panic of 1878, after which the investors sold it to Philander Smith. He ran the inn until selling it to Colonel George Alexander in 1884.

While preparing for a June grand opening after a complete renovation in 1885, Colonial Alexander was disheartened when the inn was destroyed

The Stone Bridge Inn, September 1986.

by fire. Not wanting to give up on his dream, Alexander founded the Stone Bridge Hotel and Cottage Association and rebuilt the inn, opening it in 1888. A writer with an obvious flair for hyperbole, and whose name is lost in time, wrote about his 1888 stay at the inn:

> *The southerly winds come up the Seaconnet River daily in summer between the high lands of Tiverton and the island of Rhode Island, deprived of that raw sea-damp and fogs so unpleasant at most seaside resorts, leaving the breezes soft and balmy, wooing the weary eyelids to sleep, whose power cannot be resisted, causing man to feel the beneficence of that law that makes every misery halt...*
>
> *From The [Tiverton] Heights on a clear day, what may be seen from all points seems almost a vision. To cast a glance eastward the outlook is over a wide stretch of diverse country, hills, dales, rocks, rivulets and forestlands, interspersed with evergreens, making the view charming to the eye. Nothing can equal the handiwork of Nature, which makes the richest of dyes look pale. Nature seems to spread out here simply to touch the sense of joy and help to add to the measure of boundless life. Upon these*

The rustic Adirondack-style lobby and lounge of the Stone Bridge House/Cottage/Inn, circa 1905.

The run-down and abandoned Stone Bridge Inn as seen in 1997.

"Heights" the morning star's first glimmer may be seen, and who can doubt here is where they "sang together." Here flash the first tints of the morning sun, and here shine the last rays from the gates of sunset. Here rises a low, deep murmur from the ocean. A light ripples across the firmament, as if Nature herself knows the council of all things and for the moment seems to confess her glorious purpose.

Stone Bridge Cottage became famous for its gourmet dining, said to be the equal of Delmonico's and Hoffman's of New York City. The inn changed hands several more times until the Feeney family bought it in 1921. The Feeneys and their relatives, the Neys, ran the inn successfully until 1965, when they retired from the business.

Ralph Cutillo bought the inn, restaurant and banquet facilities in 1965 from the Feeneys, and in 1985, he sold out to James Pedro, who managed the place for a while as a nightspot. Pedro sold it in 1987 to buyers who said that they wanted to build condominiums on the land. Those owners went bankrupt, leaving the inn abandoned until Pedro bought it again in 1993. His plans to restore the inn to its former glory days never materialized.

Again abandoned in 1997, the troubled property ended up in the hands of Judith Roldan of Attleboro, Massachusetts, after previous investors could not keep up payments on a loan. Under increasing pressure from the town council to raze the building, she acquiesced to the council's wishes and, at her own expense, hired a wrecking crew to do the job.

The inn stood at that site until January 1998, when the old, run-down 110-year-old building's supporting columns were ripped away by an excavator and the place collapsed with a loud groan.

A Stone Bridge Inn Reverie

This reminiscence of the old inn, written by Stephen Barker, originally appeared in a 1994 Sakonnet Times *special issue celebrating the 300th anniversary of Tiverton's founding.*

My first memories of the Stone Bridge Inn go back to when I attended the annual father-son night sponsored by the Tiverton Lions Club in the early 1950s. My great uncle, Alton Barker, had established his insurance business in a small office at the inn during the late 1930s.

Many years later, after graduation from college, I started working for my father in his insurance agency. During the week, we would walk to lunch at the inn. We sat at the old bar along with local businessmen.

The conversation varied between local gossip and world events. The bar was dimly lit and the high bar stools swayed and leaned with the sloping floors. The food was always tasty with generous portions. One of my favorites was the hamburger plate served the old-fashioned way.

The Neys and Feeneys treated the regulars like family. The waitresses I remember, Raylene Metcalf Bento and Ann Lynch, were friendly and always joined in the conversation, adding their own words of wisdom.

Buster Ney, bartender, conversationalist and amateur golfer, would entertain the crew with his antics and witticisms. Straight from the golf course, dressed in knickers, knee socks and tam, he would lean over the bar with the usual cocktail in one hand and a cigarette in the other. How he could mix a drink with both hands occupied amazed us all.

Gradually time took its toll on the inn and, as the families grew older, their interest waned and it was sold. The sagging floors, the screened porch and the old bar were removed and the charm was gone.

The Stone Bridge Inn, as many of us remember it, is gone. It is the hope of many that the inn can be preserved and maintained so that it may again be a vital part of Tiverton's heritage.

THE OLD LANDMARK INN COMES DOWN

For many years, the ramshackle Stone Bridge Inn, with its sagging roof and broken windows, looked ready to tumble down or be set on fire by vandals.

On Thursday, January 15, 1998, the 110-year-old building showed that it was tougher than most imagined. The rats were exterminated (there were not as many as some suspected), the gas was shut off and demolition was set to begin. By late morning, crews from Almeida Excavating of Brayton Road, Tiverton, had ripped away large portions of the building.

On Thursday, January 15, 1998, the 110-year-old Stone Bridge Inn became a pile of rubble.

The noisy work drew a small crowd of spectators, most aiming cameras at the proceedings. They gathered across Main Road near the parking lot of the Getty gasoline station. Police closed off the street just in case the building decided to topple west, taking power lines with it. In addition, Narragansett Electric trucks and firefighters were standing by.

The end seemed fast approaching. The inn's entire southeast corner appeared to lean on a single heavy wooden support column. Workers hitched one end of a cable to the post and the other end to a powerful diesel excavator and then stood well back. Spectators aimed their cameras while the excavator gave a mighty tug. The post snapped free, the three story building creaked and…nothing. Seagulls perched along the roof did not budge. Much discussion and maneuvering later, the crews attacked a second column. Again, the column wrenched loose, cameras clicked, the inn trembled…and held.

"It was stronger than it looked," said Ronald Almedia. "We had five beams out from under that southeast side, and it didn't go. It was starting to lean though." Stamping their feet against the cold, the sidewalk supervisors offered advice of their own.

"What they should have done is taken down all those back posts at the same time," said one man.

"You watch," said another, "the whole thing is going to slide right out onto the road."

"Look at that mural," said a woman pointing to an exposed inside wall. "Someone ought to save it."

People shared stories of "the best bar you ever saw" and good times spent with departed friends. Out by the back fence, neighbors preferred words like "firetrap" and "eyesore." They had been pleading for the restoration or demolition of the place for more than a decade.

The wrecking crew now took a more direct approach. The excavator moved in closer on its tracks and bit huge chunks from the inn, its jaws raking the building from the third floor down, loosing avalanches of shingles, glass and insulation. Another machine tugged at a cable attached near the inn's roof to prevent it from heading west. Still stubborn, the building refused to fall.

At 12:30 p.m., the crew called time out to regroup. They turned off the machine's engines and pondered their work, pointing out key beams and third-floor dormers, now at crazy angles seemingly suspended in midair. "They are going to move around to the other side and try from there," said a spectator who seemed knowledgeable. That was enough for most of the onlookers, many of whom had already watched for more than two hours.

"No way is that coming down today," said a man as he set off for his car. Disappointed at not seeing the old inn crumble to the ground, the crowd evaporated. Then, with the body of witnesses all but gone, the inn finally had had enough. The support cable snapped. Emitting a few final groans, the inn collapsed into a pile of rubble and cloud of dust. In that instant, the face of Tiverton changed forever.

"It did catch us a bit by surprise when it finally went, but it fell right where we wanted it," Mr. Almedia said. With the first step in clearing the site completed, Almeida predicted that his firm had another month of work ahead before the job was done.

Some of the beams and plywood were worth salvaging, but most of the wood was ground up on site and trucked to the landfill. Almost everything of value, including the old bar, had been removed years ago in preparation for a failed attempt at restoration.

BREEZES DINNER THEATER

According to the January 22, 1998 issue of the *Sakonnet Times*, the owners of the Breezes Restaurant claimed that theater performances did not draw customers as they had hoped. Thomas Hurrie and Melody Landary of Wareham, Massachusetts, drew the curtain closed on their dinner theater.

The restaurant and 275-seat banquet hall are doing fine, however, and remain open for business. Hurrie and Landary bought the former Almeida's family restaurant at 91–97 Crandall Road in the fall of 1997 from Joseph and Mary Lou Almeida for $340,000.

Hurrie announced that in addition to the restaurant's food and banquet business he plans to continue the property's other attractions, including the miniature golf and batting cage outside. Inside, he said, there will be a sports bar downstairs, and the dinner theater will continue there on a smaller scale. Warm weather will bring an ice cream parlor, they hope.

He is disappointed, he said, that the dinner theater idea did not draw the interest they had hoped. Starting in November and running through the holidays, the troupe of performers offered *The Odd Couple*, led by director Anthony E. Bosworth.

"It was well received," said Hurrie. "We had some people who came back two or three times." Unfortunately, he added, it did not attract enough reservations to pay the considerable costs of running the theater. Perhaps it might do better at another time of year. Director Bosworth said that an unfavorable review in the *New Bedford Standard Times* deserved much of the blame for the theater's demise.

THE RAILROAD

Although the Stone Bridge provided easy movement to and from Aquidneck Island, the town remained in the horse and buggy era until the opening of the Old Colony and Newport Railroad, connecting Fall River with Newport in 1846. A railroad station and a Western Union telegraph office were built where the railroad turned abruptly west to cross the narrow channel to Portsmouth.

From about that time, the name Tiverton was unofficially applied to the neighborhood around the station, while Stone Bridge continued to be used for the bridge area. Eventually, a plank walk connected the two places. The railroad is responsible for the transformation of the Tiverton–Stone Bridge area by making it readily accessible to several local urban centers.

In 1898, a new draw was installed on the Old Stone Bridge, and trolley tracks were laid. In 1907, a modern steel draw was built for the proposed Newport and Fall River Street Railway, which required an iron and steel structure. The new bridge provided a twenty-foot-wide roadway capable of supporting twenty tons.

The new bridge and its approaches suffered severe damage due to strong tidal flow and violent storms. Temporary closings of the old bridge forced the State Division of Highways to provide free ferry service. The bridge survived with interruptions due to ship collision damage and the hurricanes of 1938 and 1954 until May 6, 1957, when it was officially closed after 165 years of service. Traffic now turned to the new Sakonnet River Bridge a short distance north, near the steel railroad bridge.

The railroad station at Riverside Drive, Portsmouth. The Old Colony Railroad crossed the Sakonnet River about one mile north of the Stone Bridge.

The Pocasset railroad depot, circa 1920.

SAKONNET RIVER RAILROAD BRIDGE

The Old Colony and Newport Railroad built the first railroad bridge over the Sakonnet River in 1864; in 1898, it was damaged and replaced.

A modified Baltimore through truss span and a cantilevered assembly, about 220 feet long and composed of two identical trusses, spanned the

This is the old Baltimore twin-truss railroad bridge in the north end of Stone Bridge Village, circa 1900. Railroad passengers were provided service to Aquidneck Island until 1937.

Sakonnet River between Portsmouth and Tiverton. The circular track on which the bridge pivots was mounted on a central pier in the middle of the river. An engine house mounted atop the central span housed a boiler and a steam engine, which supplied the needed power; it was later electrified. Semaphore signals were located at each end of the bridge. A large steel tower carries overhead power cables ninety-five feet above the river.

In the twentieth century, the New York, New Haven and Hartford Railroad owned the line, providing passenger service to Aquidneck Island until 1937.

The bridge was closed in 1980 when it was damaged by a heavier-than-usual trainload. The final deathblow came in 1988 when a barge ran into the open bridge; the central pier was removed in 2006, and in 2007, an explosive charge destroyed the submerged remains.

THE RAILROAD'S SURVIVAL STRUGGLE

In this October 24, 1973 East Bay Window *article, Sue Weller wrote about the railroad's struggle out of the past into an uncertain future.*

"One of the most beautiful lines we have," said conductor Russell Manning of the Fall River to Newport branch of the Penn Central Railroad.

A circa 1906 view of the Tiverton approach to the Sakonnet River railroad swing bridge.

However, beauty is not what makes a railroad go, at least not anymore. The line, scheduled for abandonment by Penn Central since June, was closed for one week when new federal safety regulations took effect, because of the substandard condition of the track.

Although the single train on the line was running again and abandonment hearings were not yet scheduled, indications abound that the "end of the line" is in the future.

Serving Aquidneck Island for more than a century via the Sakonnet River railroad bridge, the line in recent decades has decreased in importance to the local economy. Around the turn of the century, the train pulled "the most luxurious cars in the world" to Newport, private cars owned by the cream of Newport's high society.

At that time part of the New Haven Line, the train functioned as a major transport vehicle for the island, carrying passengers and freight for the local resort economy. During the 1930s business slowed, but was revitalized during World War II when it serviced the Newport Naval Base with troops and supplies.

Near the war's end, the line's biggest train, the Barnum and Bailey Circus Train, traveled to Newport.

Since then, development of highway and air transportation has eaten deep into the nation's railroad business, with direct effects on the Fall River to Newport line.

Engineer John Donahue and brakeman Archie Jordan agree: "What we carry is high, wide and heavy." They explain that rail transport is cumbersome, so industry tends to avoid it except for products, which would be very expensive to ship by other means.

Rods, wire and plastic insulation for Kaiser Aluminum, lumber and hardware for Weyerhaeuser and J.T. O'Connell [building supply store], and various cargoes for the Navy Base are the mainstay of the line, but they hardly sustain it.

On a typical mid-week run to Newport, Train BX-1 pulled out of Fall River with ten "loads" and four "empties" rolling behind the engine and caboose. Archie ticked off the day's haul: a load of flour for Globe Baking Company in Fall River, five loads of lumber and four empties for Weyerhaeuser, three loads of reels for Kaiser Aluminum and a car of lumber for J.T. O'Connell in Newport.

Returning that afternoon, the train pulled only three "loads," all from Kaiser Aluminum.

"In New England, for every seven loads, four to five cars return empty," said Robert McKiernan, public information officer for Penn Central's

In this view, the two railroad trusses are turned to allow boat passage.

general offices in New Haven, Connecticut. He said the train makes a trip to Newport once each week, usually returning with an empty car for which the railroad receives no revenue. Profits are made, he explained, when the train runs loaded both directions. The train runs only as far as Kaiser on Monday, Wednesday and Friday.

Penn Central filed for abandonment of the 9.3 miles serving Newport and the navy base because of the unprofitable trip every week for a single one-way load. With reduction of naval base activity, the railroad business almost ceased.

The abandonment plan received protests from Newport, Middletown and Portsmouth officials who hoped the rail service may be utilized in the economic rehabilitation of the navy base land. Much of the area is expected to be surplussed to the state or towns, and will probably be developed as an industrial park.

THE RAIL BRIDGE'S FINAL DAYS

We learn many succinct facts from Bruce Burnett in this November 5, 1997 Bay Window article about the history and final days of the old Sakonnet River Railroad Bridge.

Anyone who thinks navigating past the Sakonnet River Railroad Bridge is a hair-raising ordeal should imagine a century ago when boaters approached that torturously narrow cut with a wall of roaring water flushing under the Old Stone Bridge.

At the rate of 100 million gallons a minute, seawater churned through the 33-foot wide channel. It is said that the water was often a foot higher on one side of the bridge than the other.

The experience wrecked vessels and cost mariners their lives. The channel's hydraulic problems attracted attention all the way down to the halls of the United States Congress and eventually developed into a states rights issue is the remembrance of Ned Connors.

With the exception of a few fishermen, Conners spent more time traipsing about the old span than anyone else.

An industrial archaeologist, Conners was hired to preserve the memory of the doomed bridge before being cut into scrap sometime in 1998 or 1999. Armed with a 4-by-5 format camera and measuring tools, he inspected every

Left: The mighty swing bridge mechanics.

Below: In this elevated photograph, you can see the new Sakonnet River Bridge construction next to the Sakonnet River railroad swing bridge.

inch of the bridge, developing a genuine respect for the structure's architect and builders along the way. He pored over the bridge's plans and gathered old photos and lore.

That lore includes tales of the death-defying days before the 1899 construction of the present bridge.

Even before construction of the previous railroad bridge in 1864, Tiverton Basin was a place respected by boaters. The nearby Stone Bridge passage of that time had an excruciatingly narrow width of only thirty-three feet and a depth of just ten feet. An extraordinary amount of water passed through that draw with every tide causing a perilous crossing for boaters.

The Old Colony Railroad wanted to build a bridge to link Aquidneck Island to the rest of the world and early plans show it running alongside the Old Stone Bridge.

Back in those days, railroads did pretty much what they wanted. Rhode Island's General Assembly was in their pocket. Rather than build next to Stone Bridge in 1864, they located that first railroad bridge further north near the site of today's Sakonnet River Bridge. There, at the swing bridge, the gap was as narrow as the Stone Bridge channel to the south, creating a double bottleneck.

Conners said it was an immediate nightmare. The twin sluiceways were hopelessly tight for the immense flow of water that wanted to get through, "Mariners avoided the place like the plague."

The federal government, which generally stayed out of state-related navigational issues, felt obliged to step in. They saw this as creating a terrific impediment to commerce. The railroad and the state resisted pressure to do something about the mess they created.

When a new swing bridge with wider sluiceways was built, the problem eased considerably. The wider, deeper channel was capable of carrying about 10 times as much water, and hurricanes ultimately helped widen the Stone Bridge slot.

THE SWING BRIDGE MATERIAL AND CONSTRUCTION

Mr. Conners wrote a detailed account of his findings, which are collectively housed in the Rhode Island Historical Resources Archive.

Though rusty and worn out, close inspection of the swing bridge reveals remarkable engineering and construction. Fabricated in sections

The new Sakonnet River Bridge from Tiverton to Aquidneck Island, the gateway to the Portsmouth Hummocks, Island Park, Common Fence Point and Newport, Rhode Island. From 2010 to 2012, a new Sakonnet River Bridge was built, replacing the old worn-out, ill-maintained bridge. A great statewide debate ensued concerning the establishment of a toll on the new bridge.

The Sakonnet River Bridge, completed in 1956. In this mid-1950s photo, the railroad swing bridge was still in use.

in Pennsylvania by the Pennsylvania Steel Company, the bridge was also erected in sections.

"It was beautifully built, very solid with sophisticated machinery," Conners said. He believed that much of the masonry was quarried out of the Hillsides of the nearby Hummocks in Portsmouth.

All of the swing section's tremendous weight rests atop an extraordinary center bearing made of phosphor-bronze, an extremely durable, low-friction material. Conner thinks that the bridge is the victim of bad press, with descriptions such as "dilapidated."

On the Portsmouth side, the steel is badly corroded, a victim of galvanic action, but in the middle and on the Tiverton side, you can rub the surface with an emery board and see like-new metal. From an industrial archaeology standpoint, the Sakonnet swing bridge is getting the full treatment from Connors, and his report is the first of its type.

COLONEL BARTON AND THE BATTLE OF RHODE ISLAND

A very important camp of the colonial American army was pitched on Tiverton Heights above the Stone Bridge during the American War for Independence while the British were holding possession of Aquidneck Island. From this point, the American army, under General John Sullivan, crossed the Sakonnet River in the movement that led to the Battle of Rhode Island.

When the British captured Newport in December 1776, the colonials presumed that the English might attempt to enlarge their sphere of occupation in the direction of either Providence or Boston. The shortest water distance between Aquidneck Island and the mainland, and therefore the most logical point for troop crossing, was Howland's Ferry. The Massachusetts General Court agreed to aid the colony of Rhode Island in erecting fortifications on the commanding ground overlooking this narrow strait, thus establishing a vital defense at this key site. The Tiverton Heights Fort was commissioned on June 28, 1777.

COLONEL WILLIAM BARTON

In a bold plot, a young Rhode Island militia officer, Lieutenant Colonel William Barton, captured the British commander of Newport forces in his nightshirt.

Colonel William Barton, a hatter by trade who made his home in Warren, enjoyed much respect by his men and was a great favorite of the citizens in

This portrait of the American Patriot General William Barton, painted circa 1780–85 by an anonymous artist, is on view at the Rhode Island Historical Society. The society also owns a later portrait of Barton painted in 1829, two years before his death.

this area. He was honored for his social qualities, his manners, his constant good humor and his patriotic zeal. The word was that he had an inexhaustible store of humorous anecdotes and bawdy stories.

As a corporal in the Rhode Island militia, Barton marched to the siege of Boston during the summer of 1775. The following March, when General Washington forced the British to evacuate the city, Barton was promoted to captain. When Barton's regiment returned home to guard Newport, in December 1776, the British seized the city, with massed regulars of redcoats and Hessians numbering about four thousand. Barton's small garrison of provincials was no match for British professionals, so he withdrew to the fort under construction at Tiverton Heights.

The same month, Barton learned of the capture of Washington's right-hand man, Major General Charles Lee. Lee was captured in the retreat through New Jersey. As was the military custom of the time, captured officers were exchanged for prisoners of identical rank; alas, the Americans had no officer of equal stature to exchange for Lee. The twenty-nine-year-old Barton, recently promoted to lieutenant colonel, was now second in command of the little fort at Tiverton.

In June, a citizen named Coffin escaped from Aquidneck Island and sought Colonel Barton at his headquarters. Coffin brought information that General Richard Prescott, commanding officer of the British forces on the island, was quartered with relatively light security at the Portsmouth farm of wealthy Quaker merchant Mr. Overing.

A few days later, a British deserter was brought to Barton, who questioned him at length. The deserter confirmed Barton's earlier intelligence that General Prescott was lodging at Overing's farm and added information about the security afforded the general. Barton spent the following week reconnoitering the area. The British, he learned, had camps at all the strategic spots along the shore, and their ships dotted Narragansett Bay from Newport Harbor to the northern part of the island.

Born and raised in the area, Barton had ample knowledge of Overing's house. It stands on high ground three-fourths of a mile inland from the island's western shore. A mile from that shore is the southern tip of the largely uninhabited Prudence Island. On Prudence, from the brush, Barton scouted the southern shore, where he could distinctly see the large, gambrel-roofed house and the lay of the approach to the house, including a brook that cut through the field beside it, empting down a gully into a tiny cove.

Enlargement from a single circa 1920 photograph forming a panoramic view seen from Tiverton Heights and Fort Barton. In the foreground are pogy boats in the Sakonnet River, in the middle ground are Portsmouth and Portsmouth Hummocks and in the background are Mount Hope Bay and Bristol's east shore. The Bristol lighthouse is on the extreme left (south).

A northern view of the Sakonnet River and Portsmouth; the Sakonnet Railroad Bridge is partly hidden by the buildings in the foreground.

In this view are seen the most northerly end of the Sakonnet River and Portsmouth at Common Fence Point. In the background are Mount Hope Bay and the gently sloping east face of Mount Hope.

In this 1998 photo taken from atop the Fort Barton watchtower, the wooden "Escape Bridge" from Portsmouth Island Park to Common Fence Point and the Mount Hope Bridge are clearly visible.

Upon compiling this intelligence, Colonel Barton conceived his daring plan to capture General Prescott and conveyed it to his commanding officer, Colonel Joseph Stanton. If Stanton would provide him with five whaleboats and allow him to gather volunteers, he would attempt Prescott's capture. Stanton agreed.

During the several days required to bring the whaleboats down from Providence to Tiverton, Barton selected four officers with unquestionable courage and patriotism. To confound the many Royalists acting as British spies, Barton's expedition to capture Prescott took a roundabout trip through Mount Hope Bay and consumed several days, recruiting a force of forty selected volunteers, all sworn to secrecy.

The five whaleboats pushed off from Tiverton on the night of July 4. Barton's boat took the lead with nine men, and each of the other four had an officer and seven men. On their way across Mount Hope Bay, a sudden thunderstorm scattered the boats. To avoid detection by British camps and ships, each boat independently rowed a roundabout route, taking them until one o'clock in the morning to reach Bristol.

The next morning, Barton took his four officers to little Hog Island, just off the coast of Bristol, where through his spyglass they could see the British encampments on Aquidneck and the ships anchored in the bay.

Barton's plan included exhaustive rowing from Bristol to Warwick Neck on the mainland opposite the northern tip of Prudence Island. From there, they would head through the narrow passage between the islands of Prudence and Patience and then hug the Prudence shore to its southern end. Finally, they would cut across the channel to Aquidneck, landing at the cove below the Overing home.[7]

He stopped in Bristol to perfect the details and in Warren to see his family. He finally rendezvoused with his stalwart party of raiders at Warwick Neck.

Barton's Daring Raid and Beyond

Lieutenant Colonel William Barton and his forty fearless raiders executed one of the most daring exploits in the records of the American military. On July 9, 1777, one year after the signing of the Declaration of Independence, the party launched its attack from the west side of Narragansett Bay. Under cover of darkness, the five whaleboats, with muffled oars, silently hugged the western shore of Prudence Island to avoid detection by British ships patrolling upper Narragansett Bay.

After quickly gaining the grounds of the Overing farm, the Continentals stealthily overpowered the sentries, broke into the house and battered down the bedroom door, rudely arousing the general from his quiet reading. Barton, with pistol in hand, informed the general, in a courteous fashion, that he was now the colonel's prisoner.

Barton's men, however, were not as courteous. They insolently jostled Prescott, clothed only in his nightshirt, outside into the night. He was hustled through stubby cornfield in his bare feet and pushed into an awaiting boat. The general was successfully transported to the Warwick shore, where he was imprisoned in a nearby house.

Upon learning of the circumstances surrounding General Prescott's capture, British lieutenant Frederick Mackenzie, adjutant of the Royal Welch Fusiliers, wrote of the abduction that it was "most extraordinary that a general commanding a body of four thousand men, encamped on an island surrounded by a squadron of ships of war, should be carried off from his quarters in the night by a small party of the enemy without a shot being fired."

Many thousands of men gathered at the Tiverton Heights fort in the summer and fall of 1777 for an October invasion of Aquidneck. However, because of insufficient time for the amassing of materiel, the inexperience of the officer in charge and the accompanying foul weather at the designated times of invasion, two halfhearted attempts to establish beachheads across Howland's Ferry were frustrated.

In the spring of 1778, General Washington selected General John Sullivan, an officer of proven ability in staging operations, for a new invasion attempt of Aquidneck. The Marquis de Lafayette was to coordinate the participation of a French fleet and landing force, and a grand plan of a strike by land and by sea was organized. On August 9, 1778, the Battle of Rhode Island began with the crossing at Howland's Ferry of eleven thousand Continental line troops and militia.

Again, the frailties of man and the unpredictable behavior of nature plagued the Rhode Island campaign. Lafayette's disappointment at a reduced role of command, the French admiral D'Estaing's failure to contribute landing troops and the severe damage sustained by the French fleet in a violent storm brought the full force of the defending British, Hessian and Loyalist troops to bear on the hardy invaders from Tiverton. Without the sea attack to draw the attention of the defenders away from the land attack, the British line held.

After a siege of twelve days by American forces dug in on Honeyman's Hill in Middletown, a weary and disappointed General Sullivan realized that the land attack alone could not penetrate the English line. With extreme regret, Sullivan was obliged to order withdrawal. Near midnight on August 30, 1778, the last of the Americans left Aquidneck. The regular troops rejoined General Washington, the militia returned home and only a small force stayed to man the guns at Fort Barton.

BARTON'S LATER CIVILIAN DAYS

Barton's fighting days ended when he received a wound in the groin during a skirmish with the British. Rhode Islanders heaped many honors on their hero; he was elevated to the rank of adjutant general of the state militia and elected to the House of Deputies.

The Continental Congress fittingly noted his heroic exploit and voiced its appreciation to Barton and his men, presenting the colonel an elaborately engraved sword. The success of this *coup de main* was of tremendous importance in boosting the low morale of the American people at that particular time in the war. It was most appropriate that the fort in Tiverton was named in honor of this soldier with outstanding patriotism and bravery.

In an effort to encourage development, the State of Vermont offered free land to veterans of the Revolution. Barton and a group of like-minded individuals joined in acquiring a township, naming it Providence. A few years after 1795, when he settled in to develop his newly acquired real estate, a split occurred among the former solders.

His former partners accused Barton of selling land that he did not own; a long and nasty court battle ensued. The court judged Barton guilty and imposed a fine. At age sixty-four and characteristically unbending, he declared the verdict unfair and refused to pay the fine. The court was unmoved and sentenced Barton to home confinement until the court levy was paid. Associates paid part of the assessment; only $272 remained unpaid, and though he was financially able to pay it, he refused.

Barton remained a voluntary prisoner for thirteen years before a rescue occurred from an unexpected source. The Marquis de Lafayette, on a triumphant tour of America, learned of Colonel Barton's predicament and sent the Vermont court his personal draft for the unpaid balance.

Now free at the age seventy-seven, Barton returned to Rhode Island and to his wife and sons. He lived another six years, stubbornly insisting, to his last breath, that the court verdict was unjust.

Scenes of Naval Engagements

Tiverton's waters were the scenes of two engagements with the enemy. Fortifications on Gould Island, then known as Owl's Nest, and at Fort Point, below Tiverton Heights, aided in covering American troops being ferried across the Sakonnet River. On a night in October 1777, Major Silas Talbot, in a small sloop, captured the blockading British row galley the *Pigot*. In July 1778, several British ships lying at anchor, including the sloop of war the *Kingfisher*, were set on fire when two French frigates entered the Sakonnet. The *Kingfisher* drifted to the foot of High Hill, where munitions on the ship exploded.

BRIDGEPORT AND NANNAQUAKET

A
lthough never precisely defined and not identified on any mid-nineteenth-century maps, Bridgeport is shown on maps of 1870 and 1895 and is cited in late nineteenth-century and later references.

The narrows leading out of Nannaquaket Pond have always been the site of various types of business activities. Sometime in the late seventeenth or early eighteenth century, Joseph Wanton settled in Tiverton. His property faced the north end of Nannaquaket Pond, where he established a shipbuilding enterprise. For a time, the pond was known as Wanton's Pond (or Cove).

Before 1700, John Gray owned one of the first taverns in Tiverton in his place along the Gut. Later, his house was the home of Tiverton's most prosperous fishing family, the Churches; a seine house and a fish-processing factory were located adjacent to the house. Reportedly, a store at this point, probably at the site of today's Manchester Seafood market, was one of the oldest buildings in town used for business. A large fish packing industry was established at Bridgeport at an early date.

Today, little remains of the old structures. The 1938 hurricane destroyed the Gray-Church House and the seine house, the old Barker House along the brook was dismantled, an icehouse built along the brook was taken down and the former schoolhouse was converted to an American Legion hall. Manchester Seafood Market still carries on here in a large wood-shingled building, with fishing boats along the dock. This is one of Tiverton's picturesque places, a reminder of the town's long relationship with the bay and the sea.

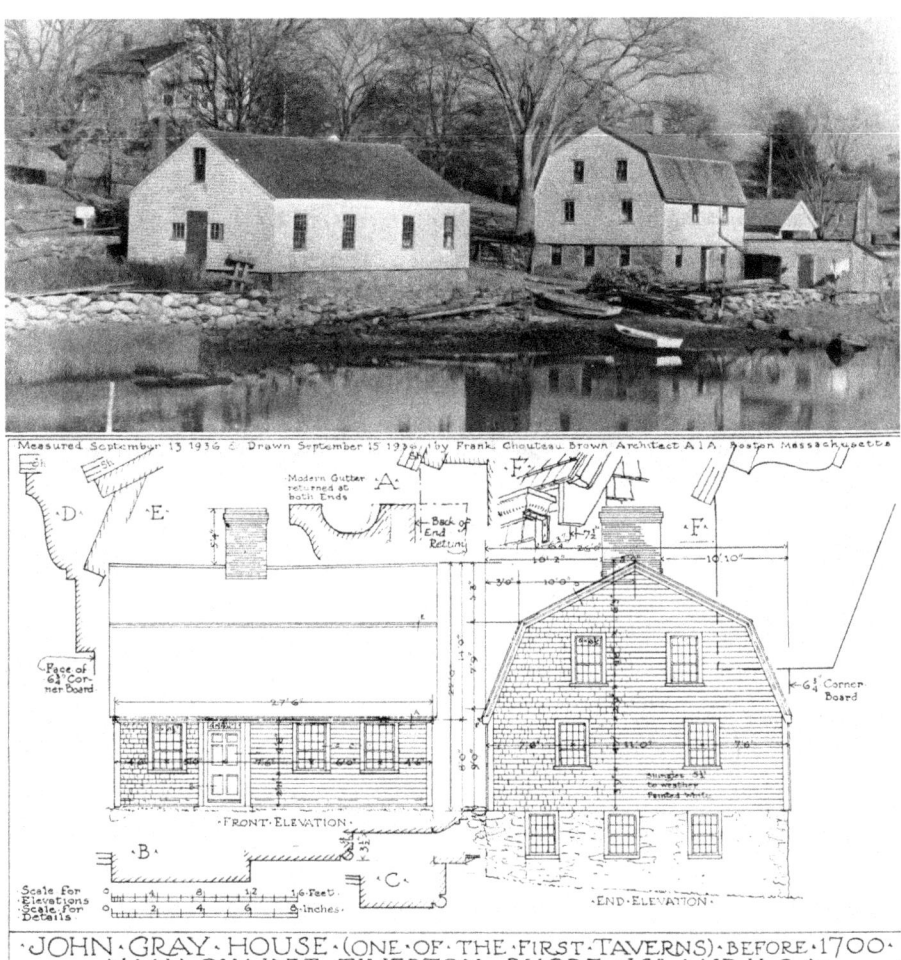

·JOHN·GRAY·HOUSE·(ONE·OF·THE·FIRST·TAVERNS)·BEFORE·1700·
NANAQUAKET·TIVERTON·RHODE·ISLAND·U·S·A·

The John Gray House (or the Gray-Church House) in Nannaquaket, near or on the site of the Manchester Seafood Market.

To the rear of the Manchester brothers' shellfish market along the Quaket River is a long dock, where fishing boats tie up and unload their catch. This landing may have been the site of Joseph Wanton's boatyard. The present building appears to be the Bridgeport Block, although the original roof and chimney have been removed and the front altered. The old Bridgeport Block was one of the first stores in town that had dwelling units above.

NANNAQUAKET NECK HISTORIC DISTRICT

This district is a residential area along the Nannaquaket Road, with several short side streets bounded by the Sakonnet River to the west, Quaket River to the north and Nannaquaket Pond to the east, in a line from the pond to the river on the south.

The Neck was originally settled by the Pocasset, a subtribe of the larger Wampanoag nation. Queen Weetamoe (wife of Alexander, the brother of King Philip, ruler of the tribe) lived here near the northern end of the Neck.

Unlike most of Tiverton, which is covered by forest, the Neck included grassland and patches of arable land where maize, beans and pumpkins grew. In 1651, several Wampanoag sachems sold the Neck, commonly called Nannaquaquit or Pogasock Neck, to Captain Richard Morris of Portsmouth. Nannaquaket Pond was then Pogasocke Pond. The deed mentions an Indian cornfield to the south and meadow ground on the east side of the pond, with timber fencing. Acquired without the consent of the Plymouth Colony, Morris reached an agreement in 1659 with the colony, recognizing his ownership of the nearly 457-acre tract. Nannaquaket Neck thus was not a part of the original Pocasset or Puncatest purchase.

In 1737, the land belonged to Andrew Oliver, the Tory lieutenant governor of Massachusetts Bay colony who was living in Boston at the time of his death in 1774. Because of his pro-British sympathies in 1775, the colony confiscated his land, except for a tract in the southern part set off for Oliver's heirs.

In 1782, the Neck was deeded to Colonel Israel Angell, Major Coggeshall, Jeremiah Olney and Captain William Tew in return for wartime service of Colonel Angell's regiments. By 1791, Jeremiah Olney and Thomas Hughes owned the land, from which the Rhode Island General Assembly conveyed 120 acres in the northern part to Captain William Humphrey, 100 acres in the center to Nathaniel Briggs and 87 acres on the southern part to John Cooke. Oliver's heirs retained the remaining 150 acres of the original tract.

It is thought that the oldest extant building is Homelands, built by Andrew Oliver in 1760. Another old residence is the Durfee Farm in the central part of the Neck. George W. Humphrey built a house on the northern part of the Neck at an early date and farmed the land. By 1872, the Neck had only about half a dozen houses, owned by wealthy and influential people.

In 1875, George Humphrey and others were authorized to build a bridge across the strait leading into Nannaquaket Pond. In 1883, a wooden structure with stone piers and abutments and a public road laid out along the Neck were completed. The original 1883 span has been replaced many times. Now, a concrete bridge set on two granite block piers carries Nannaquaket Road over the Quaket River and Nannaquaket Pond.

A House Called
Nannaquaket

The following undated monograph by H. Glenn Reed is presented here in its entirety. On July 26, 1651, a group of Rhode Island settlers and local Indian officials met on a small peninsula separating the Sakonnet River from a tiny inlet called the Quaket River in a town now known as Tiverton to negotiate a deed of sale.

B e it know [*sic*] unto all men by these presents that we Wequiquinequa and Nummampaun, Sachin and Squa-Sachin now living upon a neck of land commonly called Nanaquaquit or Pugsasuck Neck for good causes and considerations us there unto mousing [*sic*] as also in considerations of four coates of Dutch Cloath four howes & two Axes by us Received in hand have sold & do so by these presents Bargain and sell to Captain Richard Morrise of Portsmouth on Rhode Island his heirs & Executors Admer. & Assignes for ever the aforesd Neck of Land...[8]

In 1680 an affidavit was attached to the deed by Richard Bullgar testifying that, "this deponent did write ya written deed and also testifyeth and ye aforesaid neck of land was Honestly without fraud and guile bought by and sold unto sd [*sic*] Capt. Richard Morrise, that there was no excess of Drink and all things in ye bargain done with Moderation & truly Interprated doation & under stood at the signing, sealing & Delivering of the written Deed of Sale..."[9] We have no reason to disbeliever Mr. Bullgar's word.

By the mid-eighteenth century, the land had passed from the hands of Capt. Morrise's *heirs & executors Admer. & Assignes* to Andrew Oliver who was the Stamp tax Administrator for King George III. In 1775, the state of Rhode Island, anxious to exert its independence, confiscated the land from the unfortunate Mr. Oliver and sold the neck to Captain William Humphrey. Captain Humphrey in turn willed it to his son George Washington [Humphrey].[10]

George W. Humphrey gave the land to his son-in-law Captain Nathaniel Boomer Church as a wedding present. Captain Church and his new wife Mary built the house they called Nannaquaket in 1872. Unfortunately, Mary was to live there for only seven years, leaving Nathaniel a widower with three children, Elizabeth, Caroline and Ruth. He soon married Rhonda Seabury of New Bedford and had two more children, Nathaniel, Jr. and Mary. The young family shared the large house on the "neck" as well as a winter home in Brooklyn Heights, New York.[11]

Nannaquaket was a magnificent house, and in time its twenty acres included a twelve room dwelling with separate servants' quarters, a boathouse with a fully fitted dining hall on the second floor, a large pier, a stable with quarters for a groom and a large tower that was able to deliver water to all buildings as well as the extensive gardens and orchards on the property.[12] It faced three sides to sea, which was appropriate since Nathaniel was a sea-going man.

He was bought up on the sea. His father Joseph was a fisherman and he started working on his father's ship at the age of ten. His was a large family of seven boys and one girl. Later, he would join his six brothers to form Joseph Church & Sons, the largest menhaden fishing and processing company on the Eastern seaboard. But, as they said at a roast in his honor in New York on December 8, 1915, "all that comes in time."

The Captain loved parties. Of that, there is little doubt. He fitted the second story of his boathouse with hardwood floors, a large icebox, cooking facilities and an enormous circular dining table where he entertained friends and associates on a grandiose scale. He was a giant of a man, with a snow-white beard and a girth that betrayed a fondness for good food. He was a member of an eating club named The Elastic Table, which true to its name served elaborate dinners and clambakes in both Tiverton and New York. A typical menu from one of these parties (all male, of course) included Tiverton Bay oysters, celery, olives, almonds, Chicken Consommé, Maryland Tarrapin Croquettes, Grilled Sweet Potatoes, Roquefort cheeses, and Café Noir. Various champagnes, wines, and aperitifs, topped off by Camp Cigarettes and Corona Corona Cigars, accompanied this nine-course repast.[13] His guests understandingly appreciated this generosity and on one occasion presented him with a sterling silver Gorham loving cup engraved with representations of his ship and one of his factories. He was regaled with speeches and jokes about his Baptist religion, his Democratic party affiliation, and his Norman whiskers. All this was done in good fun, for as his fellow members of The Elastic Table put it, "He has the kindliness, the gentleness, and love of fellow men, that is found in real men."[14]

Captain Nat didn't always have a large house or the money to throw grand parties. He was born in a small seaside house in "the Gut" at Bridgeport and Tiverton. As noted before, he went to sea at the age of ten, worked his way up to Captain and fished for seventeen years off the coast of Florida. When the brothers Daniel, Nathaniel, Joe, Jim, Isaac, Fisher and George decided to go into business together in 1870, they commissioned the Herreshoff boatyard in Bristol, RI to build them what became the first fishing steamer in the United States, named, naturally, *The Seven Brothers*. Although they originally set their nets for food fish, they didn't take long to notice the rising demand for fish oil and fertilizer, especially in the expanding west. They saw in the lowly pogy a potential others seemed to miss. That ugly, oily, inedible trash fish had a great future in the lamps, soaps and fields of the expanding American frontier.

They bought a menhaden-processing factory up on the coast of Maine, dismantled it, and rebuilt on Common Fence Point in Portsmouth. Their sister Calista was in charge of feeding the workers. The cookhouse was at least 35-feet square and contained two large dining rooms. She sometimes served three meals a day to over three-hundred men. Her beans and brown bread were a local delicacy as was her quahog chowder. Other plants followed on Long Island and Round Pond Maine. By now, each brother has a ship of his own. Nathaniel custom designed his in Virginia. He named it the *George W. Humphrey* after his father-in-law. This large and dependable vessel steamed up and down the Sakonnet, through Narragansett Bay, into Long Island sound, as far south as Virginia, and as far north as Eastport, Maine. The Business was successful and profits were high.[15]

As proud as he was of his ships, Captain Church was equally as proud of the gardens surrounding his Tiverton home. The nearly twenty acres at Nannaquaket were planted in both formal and informal gardens, accented by various species of trees imported from different parts of the country. It was in one of these gardens that the marriage of his daughter Ruth took place

June 17, 1904. Newspaper accounts of the time report, "nothing was spared to make the occasion one long to be remembered by the 500 guests which assembled to witness one of the most elaborate and picturesque weddings held in this vicinity."[16] Special cars conveyed guests from New York, Boston, Philadelphia and New Bedford to Brightman's wharf [near the old railroad swing bridge] where they were ferried to Nannaquaket on the *Islander*, one of the Captain's steamboat fleet. The grounds were highly manicured and the house was decorated with streamers and festoons of laurel and daisies. The bride wore a "rich dress of embroidered crepe, and carried a bouquet of lilies of the valley."[17] An extravagant display of cut glass and silverware was presented in the dining room. Ruth was the only daughter to be married at Nannaquaket, but her wedding did the old house proud.

Nathaniel did not confine all his activities to the sea. In 1883, he was elected by the citizens of Tiverton to the Rhode Island General Assembly as a Democrat, the party not favored by men of the wealth and position he had obtained. The Republicans controlled the state government at that time and they were engaged in many of the same corrupt activities that some of our modern day politicians have pursued. Assemblyman Church promptly, as his friends at The Elastic Table described, "did to those 'Indians' in the Rhode Island legislature what an earlier Captain Church did to King Philip."[18] His constituents apparently liked what he was doing because the elected him to the Senate from 1885 to 1888 where he served on the committee to build the Rhode Island State House. Later, after retiring from the fisheries business, he was one of three men on the commission that built Stone Bridge, overseeing construction from the verandah of his beloved Nannaquaket.

Unfortunately, prosperity did not last forever. The American fisheries Corporation, which Nathaniel had founded and headed, became involved in a jurisdictional dispute with some of the railroad magnates who were trying to gain economic control over the entire transportation system. This and the discovery of cheap phosphate deposits in the west and Canada brought doom for the menhaden industry. By 1920 the heavy smell of the pogy factories was just a memory. The captain didn't live to see this. He passed away in 1916 and Nannaquaket was sold the following year. The property was acquired by the Roman Catholic Church in the 1930s and became known as St. James convent.

Although the water tower has been torn down and the boathouse where so many parties took place has been demolished, the property today is still one of the most scenic locations in Tiverton. The main house needs some restoration, the stable has been converted into retreat housing, and the gardens are not nearly so grand. Nevertheless, it is still a beautiful place for a wedding. On May 14, 1994, Benjamin Church Reed and Martha Hart were married near the site where his grandmother took her marital vows. The scale was smaller, no railroad cars were hired to transport guests, but the scene was just as lovely. One could almost hear Captain Nat roar his approval.

FOUR CORNERS AND THE OLD WHIPPING POST

I ts name is appropriate, its history is intriguing and it has the distinction of being on the country's National Register of Historic Places.

In 1683, a four-rod highway was laid out north of Four Corners; originally an Indian trail following the course of the great West Road, this later became Main Road. Records of the Puncatest proprietors dated February 24, 1683, state how the Four Corners intersection came into being:

> *We laid a highway from the highway across Captain Church's land beginning at the mill dam, we laid it four rod wide and to run from the dam to the way that is ordered by Pocasset Purchasers across their great lots to Freetown* [Fall River].
>
> *Also at forty rods north from Captain Church's land we laid a way from the way that goeth out of Puncatest east into the woods as he has the lots run of six rods wide.*

The Tiverton Four Corners Historic District, now on the National Register of Historic Places, is the focal point at the crossroads of Main Road and Puncatest Neck Road, in the southwest part of town. It was the natural point of assembly for colonial troops during the Revolution. In June 1776, Colonel Pardon Gray asked Lieutenant Philip Cory to assemble men at the corners in preparation for the arrival of French forces before the Battle of Rhode Island.

All of the noteworthy structures in the district lie along Main Road, beginning in the north at the Amicable Congregational Church and heading south to beyond the Davenport House. The buildings range in age from a circa 1730 residence to a circa 1960 commercial-industrial building. Included are eight houses, a church, a parsonage, a library, a store, a former store, a former grange hall and several industrial, commercial and professional buildings. The later groups are clustered along and near Borden Brook south of the crossroads.

The village of Tiverton Four Corners began in about 1710, partly because of the earlier settlement and growth of Puncatest and other settlements along the Sakonnet Shore. In the late seventeenth century, the proprietors of Puncatest laid out lots extending from the Sakonnet River east to Acoaxet, and the area was settled by people from Dartmouth and other nearby towns.

In 1710, a committee from Sakonnet and Puncatest measured and bounded an eighty-acre mill lot, including a mill already owned by Joseph Taber, and staked out a new mill on the site. At that time, the mill and village were called "Momscot" for the local pond (now Nonquit). Thirty building lots were also laid out at that time; these constituted the nucleus of the village of Tiverton Four Corners.

In about 1715, a member of the Almy family established a ferry at Fogland, operating for more than two centuries thereafter. Several wharves and landings along the Sakonnet Shore at Puncatest Neck contributed to the growth and prosperity of Four Corners. The Dartmouth and Westport Road was a principal east–west artery for travel, allowing a connection via ferry with Portsmouth and Newport on Aquidneck Island. A tavern had been established somewhere along the Dartmouth Road by 1749, a store was started at the southwest corner of the crossroads and a windmill was in operation in the northwest angle of the crossroads in 1776. In 1789, there were at least three dwellings and two stores, known as "the white store" and "the red store," at the crossroads.

The development of these crossroads as an important center of local "downtown" activity dates from the last quarter of the seventeenth century. In total, seventeen buildings make up the list of historic structures at Four Corners. An additional category includes eleven more buildings, both commercial and residential, dating from the Victorian period to the mid-twentieth century.

Early in the nineteenth century, the Four Corners exploded with growth. In 1808, the Amicable Congregational Society built a meetinghouse, and in 1820, a library association and United States Post Office were established. Early in the century, a hat-making manufactory established a business near Borden's Brook. In about 1847, William Pitt Bateman purchased a mill site at Borden's Brook and built a gristmill there; he also built a store and wheelwright shop with lathes and sundry machinery. At the time, this immediate vicinity was known as Pittsville. In 1876, Andrew P. White purchased buildings at Pittsville, where he erected a store at the crossroads. By 1880, the Four Corners Village was a bustling business center with farmers, dressmakers, blacksmiths and storekeepers selling various dry goods and necessaries.

In the late nineteenth century, Four Corners Village acquired several wharves constructed at Puncatest Neck. Two Providence steamers provided needed service, delivering supplies and shipping local produce to Providence markets and several local ports. The Fall River and Little Compton Stage provided daily mail service.

In the early twentieth century, fishing activities ceased, farming declined and steamer service ended. New macadam-surfaced roads and automobile traffic began playing the primary role in transporting goods and travelers. In the late 1920s, Main Road was reconstructed, and many of the colonial-era stone walls lining the roads were taken down. During the century, activities around Borden's Brook all but ceased, though gradually. The grange society was the last of the nineteenth-century activities to end, disbanding in the late 1970s.

Despite a few intrusions, the district retains a good sampling of structures from the mid-eighteenth century: the Chase-Cory House (1730), the Arnold Smith House (1750), the Soule-Seabury Mansion (1770–1809) and the A.P. White Store (1875). All well preserved and maintained, they now house professional offices, specialty clothing, art galleries and antique and dry goods shops.

CHASE-CORY HOUSE

The Chase-Cory House is a gambrel-roofed, wood-shingled cottage with an asymmetrical four-bay façade, a large brick center chimney and a four-light transom over the entrance; there are several outbuildings. The house is set above the road behind a granite block wall of quarried stone. It is believed that either Benjamin or Abner Chase built the house. This is a fine example

The Chase-Cory House (circa 1730) at 3908 Main Road, seen here in November 1996, is the location of the Tiverton Historical Society. This is a gambrel-roofed cottage with a large brick center chimney, a four-light transom over the central entrance, an asymmetrical four-bay façade and an ell at the rear. It is one of the best-preserved examples of a modern colonial-era farmhouse in Tiverton.

of a modest colonial-era farmhouse, and it is one of the best preserved of the style extant in Tiverton.

The house remained in the Cory family from 1816 until 1962. The Corys were one of Tiverton's several whaling families, including Andres and his sons, Andrew Jackson and Edward Gray, who were whaling ship captains.

The Tiverton Historical Society purchased the house in 1964 and restored it; it is now a museum and the society's headquarters.

CHASE-CORY HOUSE PHENOMENA

The following was written by Ken DeCosta in June 2012.

I would like to give you some of the background/insights into our investigations of the Chace-Cory House.

Our organization, the Rhode Island Society for the Examination of Unusual Phenomena, or RISEUP, bases its investigations of legends, folklore or reputedly haunted locations squarely on historical research and applied science. Our interest has brought us to Fort Adams, Belcourt Castle and Rose Island Lighthouse in Newport; Fort Barton in Tiverton; the Paine House Museum; the Nathanael Greene Homestead in Coventry; and the Sprague Mansion in Cranston. These are the Rhode Island sites of the 20-plus locations throughout the country listed in the National Historic Register we have had been welcomed into.

Our first trip to the Chace-Cory House was in January 2010. Our purpose for being there was strictly academic. There had been no claims of anything paranormal occurring there, but being avid history buffs we wanted to tour the location and determine for ourselves if perhaps there was some "attachment" to the home by some of its former inhabitants.

Our first night there proved to be rather interesting. EVPs, or Electronic Voice Phenomena, is a method investigators use to attempt contact with those who have passed on. Simply put, using a digital or analog recorder, investigators will ask a series of questions and in the best scenario they will hear a voice respond on playback that is not audible at the time the session is conducted.

While in the downstairs bedroom, we performed an EVP session and on playback clearly heard a female voice saying "Wake up!" No females in our team were present that evening. As we continued our experiment in that room, we again heard the same female voice, this time with a pronounced laugh. Perhaps she was amused by our efforts.

The most profound occurrence there happened as we were conducting our final session of the night, a "vigil," in which we simply sit quietly and listen to the natural sounds of the house to determine which are real, or what we might consider out of the ordinary. One of our investigators was sitting at our video monitor, where he can view all surveillance cameras set up throughout the location during an investigation. The cameras are of the infrared (IR) variety and can "see" in the dark. He found an old spoon sitting on a shelf in the foyer; he picked it up and was absent-mindedly playing with it until the session ended and personnel switched. He placed the spoon back on the shelf and swapped places with another team member.

About 25 minutes into our next session, one of our people was sitting in the "cooking area" which contains a large fireplace and table. The rest of the group was dispersed to other areas. It was then that everyone in the home heard the unmistakable sound of something metallic hitting the wooden floor in the room where the team member was sitting. As we converged on his location, we observed him checking under his chair. With a puzzled expression on his face, he turned to us and said something had landed underneath him. Turning our flashlights on it, we were amazed to see that it was a silver spoon. The investigator who had previously been sitting at the monitor said nothing but excused himself for a moment and returned to tell us that the spoon he was fiddling with earlier was missing from the shelf and identified it as the one now on the floor. The investigator who had been sitting in the chair was on camera the entire session and at no point did he change position or move from it. The object had seemed to travel by itself from one room to another!

Interestingly, when we reviewed the video from the room, in one frame we clearly see a shiny object reflecting off the infrared lighting as it suspends in mid-air before landing on the floor. This was our proof that something was indeed quite "different" about the Chace-Cory House. We have returned there on multiple occasions and we continue from time to time to record and observe some strange occurrences. We do not regard it as a "haunted house," but merely a historically significant location that may contain some residual energy from those who once called it home.

ARNOLD SMITH HOUSE: 3895 MAIN ROAD

This is a small, shingled, gambrel-roofed cottage with a central entry and a four-light transom in a three-bay façade. The house is set on a slight rise. About 1820, a long, one-and-a-half-story ell was added on the west side; later, the center chimney was removed.

SOULE-SEABURY MANSION: 3852 MAIN ROAD

Doris Seabury Soule captured a British spy in the kitchen of her house, which was in the process of being built by Abner Soule.

The Soule-Seabury house is a fine, two-and-a-half-story, five-bay façade, colonial-era residence with a hip roof and corner quoins. It features a pair of large interior brick chimneys and a central entry with transom and side lights. The house at the junction with East Road is set back from the road on a large corner lot. An iron rail fence and stone walls surround the lot. Abner Soule, a blacksmith, Revolutionary War soldier and whaler, built the house.

In 1808, Abner gave most of the homestead farm to his son, Cornelius (1769–1818). Cornelius was engaged in the China trade and involved in John Jacob Astor's plan to build a fur trading empire in the Pacific Northwest. In 1816, Cornelius deeded the house to his cousin, Cornelius Seabury (1769–1844), for payment of debts. Seabury was a merchant with business interests in Boston and Newport; he later made a successful seal hunting expedition to the Indian Ocean.

ANDREW P. WHITE STORE: 3883 MAIN ROAD

This handsome two-and-a-half-story commercial building has a bell-cast mansard roof with a cupola and a bracketed cornice above a one-story porch running the full length of the front of the building and part of the left side. The building is set close to the Main Road at the junction with Neck Road. There is a large general store on the ground floor and residences above. Mr. White, for a time the owner of the mill and icehouse at nearby Pittsville, built this store in 1875. It also housed the Four Corners Post Office.

THE WHIPPING POST

At this intersection, still marked by two old houses and two stores on the southeast corner, sits the old whipping post—a flat stone slab, only a few inches thick and standing about six feet out of the ground; it was much used by Judge Almy between 1719 and 1812. According to local tradition, the whipping post saw use especially for punishment of disobedient or lazy slaves.

The following monograph by an unknown author, titled "The Shameful Secret of the Four Corners Women," appeared in *Al's Almanac* (vol. 1, no. 1) on May 1, 1996. The almanac, produced by Lees Supermarket, is an informal and free biweekly paper:

> *There are few who reside in Tiverton, Rhode Island and the surrounding area that have not, at one time or another, experienced at first hand a convention of that town. On a warm summer day when you are en route to*

A close-up image of the old stone whipping post and sign on the John Almy House at Tiverton Four Corners. The house was torn down in the 1950s, and the whipping post was removed across the street as a stand-alone pillar—a reminder of the days of corporal punishment.

or from Little Compton or Tiverton beaches or just out for a pleasant drive along winding tree-lined roads, you will inevitably end up at Tiverton Four Corners and be "obliged" to stop and sample the popular local delicacy known as Gray's Ice Cream.

The parking lot of Gray's Ice Cream Store is invariably crammed with carloads of happy vacationers who have likewise fallen prey to that same convention, but no one seems to mind. The scene is one of family and friends and good old country fun. It would be difficult to imagine that on this spot, 200 hundred years ago an event of much import that is more serious was unfolding.

Long ago, Four Corners was the "downtown" section of Tiverton, the place where the major farm roads converged, and the location of the two general stores. From approximately 1719 to 1812, on the land, which is now Gray's parking lot at the southeast corner of the Four Corners intersection, there stood a lone upright stone post. It was not meant to support a mailbox, as the postal service of that era was far from sophisticated; nor was it a hitching post, for it was too large and angular to easily accommodate a horse's reins.

In 1797, the John Almy house was erected on the same lot. The stone pillar remained carefully preserved in its original location. To the early citizens of Tiverton this was not unusual at all as the post served as a most sacred purpose to the townspeople—the public whipping post.

For a span of almost one hundred years, the court of Tiverton meted out justice with an iron hand, sparing no one, male or female, from the possible sentence of public reprisal at the whipping post.

The following items are from original records written by John Almy (1681–1767).

"Court held at my owne house, in Tiverton, the same being in possession of Herbert C. Almy, Fogland Road Tiverton.

"Memorandum—December ye 6th, 1718:

"At a COURT held at my house in Tiverton Sohena Hope Complt Against Ruth Cashaway Indians both of Tiverton &c: Both parties being present. Ye Complaint Made Oath yt ye sd Ruth Cashaway did very much abuse her Strikening of her sd Susanah on her head & face & yt it was on ye Lords Day and Mergory Cashaway & Robby Zakorin made oath to ye Above written as Also ye Sd Ruths own Confession—it is Considerable yht the Said Ruth is Sentenced to pay a fine of five shillings or be whipped Seven lashes on her naked back laid on: for Breach of Sabath & to pay a fine of three shillings & four pence or be whipped five lashes on her Naked back for a Breach of ye peace & to pay cost of prosecution & so Stand Committed until sentence be performed. Cost allowed 12/2 Job Almy Justice Ps"

"Memorandum—December ye 6th, 1718:

"Then recd of Ruth Cashaway 5 Shilling: for breach of Sabath; & ¾ for breach of ye peace—Job Almy Justice Ps"

"Memorandum—July 7, 1772:

"It appearing by Nathan Tobes own confession that he was Drunk for which I sentence him to pay a fine of five Shillings or to be Whipt teen lashes on his naked back well laid on. And it also appearing that time Jane his wife brought them Rum into the fields the time when her arm was hurt for which I do also Sentence her to be whipt teen lashes on her Naked back well aid on.

"Per My Job Almy jjss

"The above Sentences are all satisfied by Whipping."

These incidents serve to set the stage for that fateful incident which occurred at the place that is now Gray's parking lot. It was after the American Revolution and before the War of 1812 that a woman was bound to the stone whipping post. Although she was not the first of her gender punished in this manner, her name unlike the aforementioned has not been noted for posterity.

She stood with back bared, terrified and ashamed, softly bemoaning her plight and no doubt ruing the unfortunate circumstances, which had brought her to such a sad state of affairs. All around her thronged the ladies of Four Corners in various attitudes of distress, denouncing in much greater volume than she the outrage about to inflict upon one of their own kind.

Nearby stood the sheriff who had been appointed by the court to do the flogging, eyeing the scene with a practiced air of detached indifference. In addition, idling around were men who seemed a little amused at the clamorous display of the womenfolk and more than a little interested in the shapeliness of the victim's back.

This then, was the sight that first met the eyes of the Governor as he rode homeward by way of Tiverton Four Corners—a sight which would have set a lesser man to prod his mount in the opposite direction in all due haste. However, Isaac Wilbour was a man of substantial character, being the only man from Sakonnet who ever sat in the Governor's Chair, was sent to congress and appointed to the State Supreme court. He was a good and honest Quaker, dedicated to the law and to justice, and so he rode on calmly with not a hint of astonishment in his smooth features.

As the Governor approached, the noise of the crowd grew to a deafening roar. The ladies recognized him and, flooding out into the road, barred his way. They surrounded his horse in a wave of angry churning humanity and demanded to know just what was the meaning of this! The ladies were not averse to severe tongue-lashings to keep errant members of their sex within the confines of propriety, but have a lady's back exposed and bloodied in public for a little harmless mischief making—that was too much to be borne!

The Governor listened patiently to the ladies' complaint and nodded sympathetically. Slowly he reached into the pocket of his frock coat and withdrew a booklet containing the laws of Rhode Island. After turning *several pages with great deliberation, during which time the crowd murmured expectantly, Isaac found the section he wanted and read aloud: "The condemned shall be tied to an upright post and flogged according to the sentence of the court." Then he closed the volume with an air of finality, slipped it back into his pocket, and solemnly told the women that this was the law and that as Governor he has sworn an oath to uphold the law.*

They roared their disapproval as with one voice. If that was law, then the law was not just and the Governor, as a minister of said law, had already outstayed his welcome, Isaac Wilbour was not riffled in the least. With a poise born of inner serenity and hard-earned wisdom, he leaned from the saddle and in the softest whisper, addressed those women closest to him: "But ladies, if it happened that there was no upright post, how could the law be carried out?"

For a moment, the atmosphere was electrified and then the ladies of Tiverton and Four Corners were galvanized into action. They shoved aside the unfortunate sheriff, as if he were a mere fly in a sweet ointment of their revenge—indeed, after one look into the eyes of those emboldened angels of mercy, said sheriff lifted not a finger to stop them. They swarmed upon the victim and unbound her from the post, restoring both clothes and dignity in one fell sweep. And then, with the limitless strength born of righteous fury, those women did huff and puff and push and shove and pull and drag until that "upright" post showed a definite slant! With a cry of triumph, the women gave one more mighty final effort and the post fell with a loud crash, never to rise again.

Rhode Islanders owe a great debt to Isaac Wilbour and the women of Four Corners for from that day forward, no women has ever again been publicly flogged in the State of Rhode Island.

As we read in the court records, Ruth Cashaway received a sentence of seven lashes for fighting on the Sabbath and five lashes for breach of the peace; luckily, she was able to pay the alternative fine of eight shillings and four pence. Jane Tobes was not as fortunate and suffered ten lashes "well laid on" for bringing rum to her husband in the fields.

From the viewpoint of a much more permissive society, we certainly judge these punishments as extreme. To twenty-first-century eyes, the punishments hardly fit the crimes; in fact, to us they are not crimes at all. Perhaps in a much smaller way, the Tiverton women were awakening to the absurdity of their judicial system and to the very real need for social change. It may be that they were just reacting to a situation that had become intolerable to them. As they had no substantial voice in government, their only recourse was to take matters into their own hands, and quite literally, that is exactly what they did.

Governor Wilbour, who for his part had precipitated the unusual turn of events, was indeed an open-minded and progressive man. The reader should not take Wilbour's mild reaction to the situation as leniency; Wilbour was not soft in matters of justice. Yet he was not at all concerned that "due process of law" could not be served, perhaps because he had seen too many atrocities inflicted upon the innocent in the name of justice.

As a Quaker, Wilbour was assuredly aware of the numerous persecutions suffered by his fellow Quakers and Jews at the hands of fanatics who clothed themselves with false righteousness in the robes of the law. Many Quakers were persecuted while visiting friends and relatives in neighboring colonies, but in Rhode Island, the greatest measure of religious freedom was enjoyed. In Rhode Island, freedom is the legacy of Roger Williams, Rhode Island's founder, a freedom perpetuated by those far-sighted social administrators who followed in his path.

Isaac Wilbour, as one of these, was only dong his part to keep his beloved state free from the quagmire of social injustice that springs from ignorance, narrow-mindedness and misguided religious and political fervor. It is certain that deep in the heart of that gentle public servant reposed the hope of discipline without debasement, community without forfeit of individual rights and a little understanding peaceful coexistence for all.

The area now is a quaint remnant of an earlier easygoing rural village. The old stone whipping post exists on the southwest corner of Four Corners as a stand-alone upright post.

SIN AND FLESH BROOK

In the spring of 1676, an event in the vicinity gave the chilling name to the brook flowing westward from the Fish Road area and emptying into Nannaquaket Pond at the foot of Highland Road.

Zoeth Howland, a devout Quaker, was on his way to Newport from his Dartmouth home when six Indians, one named Manasses, accosted him. Without provocation, the Indians, thought to be Sakonnets, butchered the poor man and threw his mutilated and dismembered body into the brook. When his horrified friends discovered Howland's body, they called the previously unnamed brook Sinning Flesh Brook, now corrupted into Sin and Flesh Brook.

The Bridgeport Historic District is a small area south of Stone Bridge, including the lower part of Sin and Flesh Brook, Bridgeport Road and a short portion of Main Road. Included in the district is Manchester Seafood, a former schoolhouse, a residence and a seine house along the Gut, as well as several sites along Sin and Flesh Brook.

Sometime before 1700, John Gray operated one of the first taverns in Tiverton, that place being along the Gut. Later, his house became the home of the Church family. Suspicions are that a seine house and even a fish factory were located neighboring the house. Further, records show a store at the site of today's Manchester Seafood Market, one of the oldest business buildings in town.

In about 1846, a schoolhouse joined the other buildings along Bridgeport Road, across from the Gut. Near the end of Sin and Flesh Brook, a short

In the foreground of this circa 1907 photo is the stone-walled Snell Bridge. A sawmill and a gristmill were built along Sin and Flesh Brook by Moses and Aaron Barker. In about 1844, Sylvanus Nickerson built a thread mill here.

In this 1914 photo, Highland Road winds above Sin and Flesh Brook. The two-and-a-half-story building in this photo appears to be a residence; it may have been the house used as a hospital by the French during the Revolution.

The Bridgeport area at Sin and Flesh Brook in a January 1997 photo. The Gut is at the bottom of the Brook, east of Nannaquaket Pond, and the Snell Bridge is at middle right.

Highland Road crosses the Snell Bridge at Sin and Flesh Brook. The mill burned down in about 1864 and was never rebuilt. There was an icehouse along a dammed pond created on the brook. Today, little remains except stone ruins and cellar holes, seen here in January 1997.

watercourse empties into the Gut at Highland Road. A sawmill and a gristmill were built along the brook by Moses and Aaron Barker. Later, in about 1844, Sylvanus Nickerson, who settled in Tiverton, built a thread mill here. Nickerson operated the mill until his death in 1857. Nickerson's family sold the mill to Oliver Chase and Samuel Thurston, who ran it for a few years. Daniel T. Church purchased the property in about 1861 and made improvements to the dam and mill. French solders used an old house in the area as a hospital during the Revolutionary War.

Little is left of the old structures that existed along Sin and Flesh Brook. The 1938 hurricane destroyed the Gray-Church House and the seine house, the old Barker House along the brook was dismantled, the icehouse built along the brook was taken down and the former schoolhouse was converted to an American Legion Hall. The thread mill in the general area burned down in 1864 and was never rebuilt. During the 1870s, the French hospital house was dismantled and reconstructed in Newport. Today, there remains a small building still standing, in poor condition, and there are also a few stone cellar holes and random stone foundations.

WEETAMOE WOODS

The forest of Weetamoe Woods is classified as coastal oak-holly, a natural community of oaks and American holly trees found in coastal areas of southern New England. A different forest type is found north of the sawmill and along Borden Brook below the milldam. This forested swamp includes stands of Atlantic white cedar trees. Cedar swamps were once common along the Eastern Seaboard but logged extensively in colonial times for the valuable cedar wood. These swamps are now rare and many of the surviving ones are protected. The 650 acres of Weetamoe Woods is a "middle aged" forest, with some trees that survived the 1938 Hurricane now 100–125 years old. A mature, unfragmented forest of this size is excellent habitat for canopy nesting birds that require deep woods, such as the veery, worm-eating warbler, wood thrush and Baltimore oriole. Raptors frequenting Weetamoe include barred and horned owls, and red-tailed hawks; whitetail deer, opossum, raccoon, fox, coyote, chipmunk, eastern grey and red squirrels also live in this forest. A vigorous amphibian community is present, including salamanders, wood frogs and peepers. Each year they signal the beginning

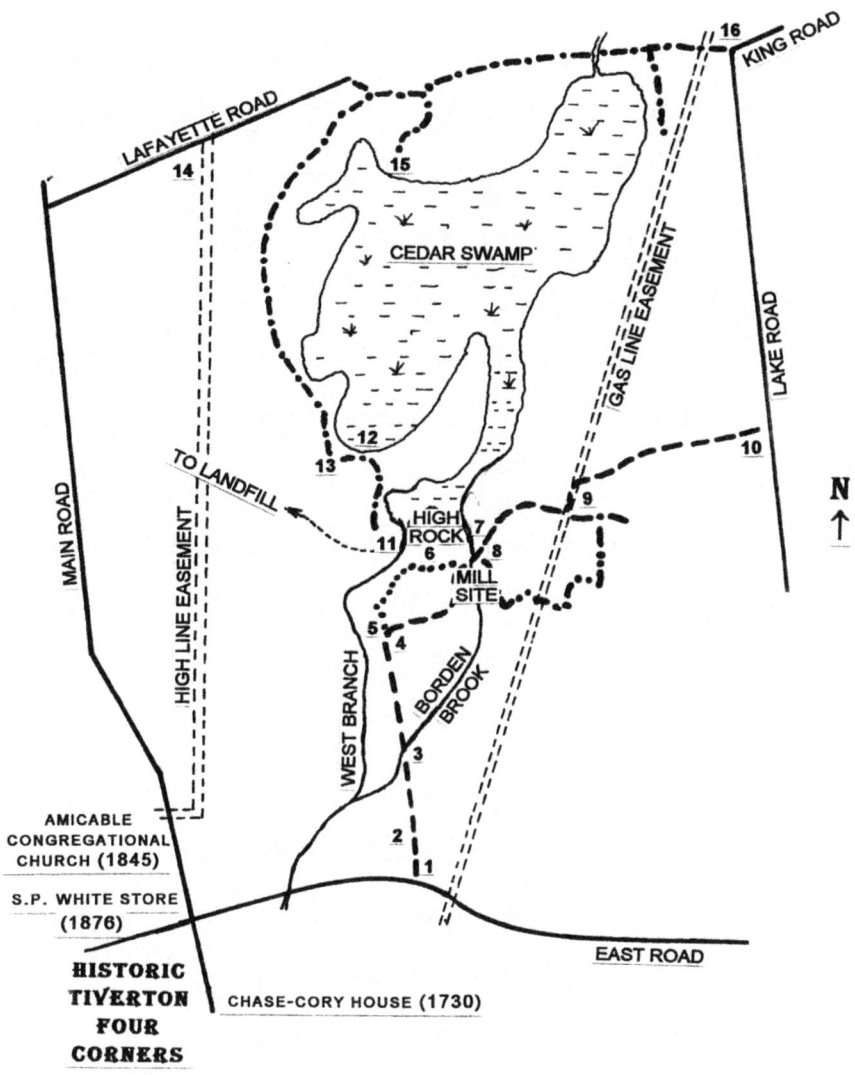

A trail map of Weetamoe Woods. (1) Eight Rod Road; (2) Squire Chase Farm; (3) Borden Brook and Slab Bridge; (4) Mill Workers' Lot; (5) Wordell Trail; (6) Base of High Rock; (7) Old Mill Site with Arched Bridge; (8) Beginning of Violet Trail; (9) Walled-in Farm Site; (10) Lake Road; (11) Beginning of Yellow Trail; (12) Walled-in Settlers' Lot; (13) Giant Oak Tree; (14) Lafayette Road; (15) Wildcat Rock and Hemlock Forest; and (16) Parking, Entrance/Exit.

No wooden structures remain in Weetamoe Woods. The visitor will find crumbling stone walls, foundations and cellar holes. This photo is the cellar hole and part of the foundation for Sharpen Almy's homestead.

of spring with their raucous mating chorus that can be heard from the vernal pools in the area. Weetamoe Woods is not only a forest. Twelve acres of grassland are being managed on former plow land that abuts Eight Rod Way to the east. This creates favorable conditions for ground nesting birds such as bobolinks, eastern meadowlarks, and savannah sparrows. All of these birds are in decline in the East. Grasslands also provide habitat for insects, butterflies, and food for raptors such as the American kestrel that feeds on meadow voles and deer mice found in open fields.

The Weetamoe Woods, here described by the Tiverton Open Space and Land Preservation Commission, is the site of the Borden's Brook Sawmill. The site today includes the remains of the milldam, millrace and mill foundation, constructed of large, irregularly shaped and odd-sized granite blocks. A rough wooded road near the mill site crosses the brook over a twelve-foot-wide stone arch bridge, restored in the mid-1990s. In the late nineteenth century, John Gray and Joseph Seabury operated the mill.

THE POCASSET CEDAR SWAMP FIGHT

Before this dense forested swamp obtained the name Weetamoe Woods, locals referred to it as the Pocasset Cedar Swamp. This place was the scene of a battle in King Philip's War.

One of Tiverton's wild, impenetrable and uninhabitable swampy tracts was the site of an encounter between colonists and Indians. The engagement at Pocasset Swamp came at the end of an eighteen-day clash that began in the southern part of Tiverton. The Indians fought their way northward and, on July 18, 1675, ambushed the pursuing English force from the swamp. After falling back, the colonial troops advanced into the swamp but quit their attack at nightfall. During the night, Philip, Weetamoe and the most able warriors crossed the Taunton River and escaped into central Massachusetts, leaving behind about one hundred wigwams and as many men who were taken captive.

In all, sixteen whites were killed, and the Indians suffered "heavy losses" in what has become known as the Battle of Tiverton.

EIGHT ROD HIGHWAY

Laid out in the eighteenth century, Eight Rod Highway runs in a north–south direction through the center of present-day Tiverton into Fall River. Today, part of the old road is heavily wooded and is lost in Weetamoe Woods; part of the old road is also incorporated into Fish Road. In the southern part, north of East Road, it is lined by crudely laid stone walls. An old stone bridge carries the road over a small brook and a foundation along the east side of the road, just south of where the road makes a sharp turn to the east. Originally, the road marked the easternmost line of the Pocasset land purchase; the largest lots extended from the Sakonnet River to this highway.

A rod is a British unit of measure. The intention of building the original eight-rod width was so twenty British soldiers could march in a line shoulder to shoulder.

LITTLE COMPTON

A HISTORICAL PROSPECTIVE

Little Compton is a fishing village, summer resort and community unspoiled by the hand of time. Here are the home and grave of Betty Alden, John and Priscilla Alden's daughter who married schoolmaster William Pabodie and here are homesteads whose occupants bear the original names of Rhode Island pioneers. Originally an Indian hamlet, here in early days the female sachem Awashonks sided with the English against Metacomet, chief sachem of the Wampanoags.
—*anonymous, 1936, scrap clipping*

The General Court at Plymouth favored early settlers of the colony; the court considered the Sakonnet lands included within its jurisdiction and distributed parcels to "old freemen" and then to children born or reared in Plymouth Colony. In the wisdom of the court, the granting of land constituted a policy as compensation to settlers who suffered hardship during the colony's early years.

On July 30, 1673, Constant Southworth and others received from Queen Awashonks a deed for a large tract of land in the western part of her realm, roughly a four-and-a-half-square-mile area. The Sakonnet petitioners met in July 1673 to establish articles of association. The men who became proprietors agreed to several conditions of land ownership. A proprietor could not appropriate more than two parcels of land upon penalty of forfeiting the excess to the company, nor could he dispose of his land to a

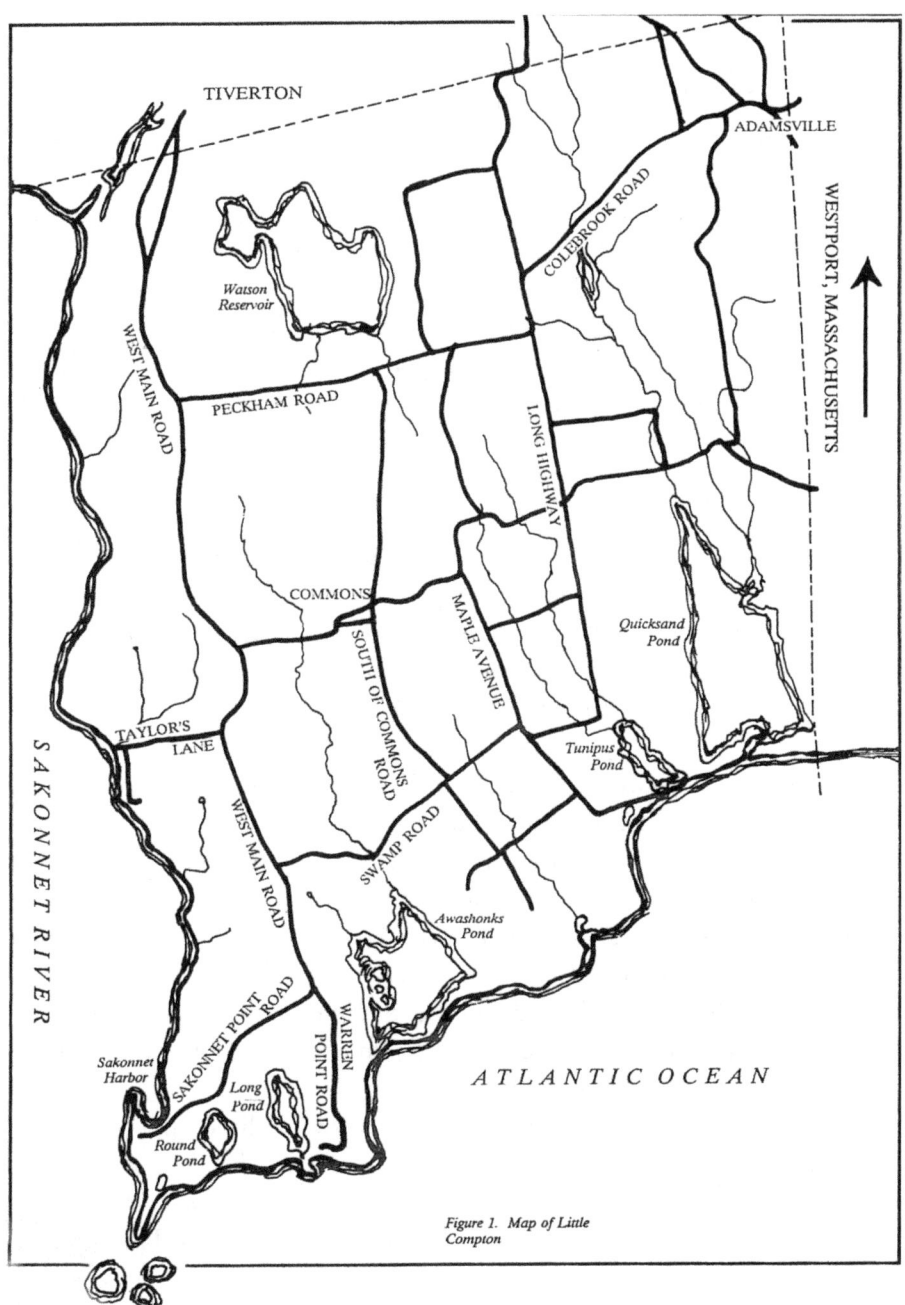

Figure 1. Map of Little Compton

A topographical map of Little Compton, drawn in 1990.

person not related to him without majority consent of the company. This strict rule reflected the desire of the colony to decrease land speculation.

The Plymouth General Court declared the Sakonnet lands a township in 1674. In April of that year, the proprietors assembled in Duxbury, paid their dues and drew lots for the first purchase. Benjamin Church had interest in the company represented by Southworth. As written in the chapter on Church, over the course of several years he acquired large tracts of real estate. The first permanent settlement in the deeded lands was by Benjamin Church in 1674. Except for Benjamin Church quickly occupying his purchase, it is unknown how soon others followed him to build farmsteads.

Church wrote the following in his memoir:

I was the first Englishman that built upon that neck which was full of Indians. My head and hands were full about settling a new plantation, where nothing was brought to. No preparation of dwelling house or out-house fencing made. Horses and cattle were to be provided, ground to be cleared and broken, and the utmost caution to be used to keep myself free from offending my Indian neighbors all around me.

Located in the southeast corner of Rhode Island, Little Compton is a rough trapezoid slightly more than twenty-three square miles, which together compose just over 2 percent of the state's land area. With S'connet Point at its southwest, Little Compton juts into the Atlantic Ocean at the mouth of the East Passage of Narragansett Bay, also known as the Sakonnet River. While more than half of the town's border is coastal, the absence of a deep natural harbor has long discouraged intense maritime development, although a small commercial fleet of independent clam, lobster and finfish fishermen work out of S'connet Point.

Water within the town is largely still and provides little opportunity for transportation or industrial use. Located on the south shore are several saltwater coastal ponds, separated from the ocean by barrier beaches: Quicksand Pond, Tunipus Pond, Long Pond and Round Pond. The 225-acre Briggs Marsh complex is historically valuable as a wildlife preserve—one of the best spots in the state for migratory Canada geese. The only natural freshwater pond is Simmons Pond, fed by Cold Brook, which drains into Quicksand Pond in the northeast part of town. The Watson Reservoir, near the Tiverton town line, is manmade. The few brooks—Adamsville Brook,

Cold Brook, Sisson Brook and Dundury Brook—are all shallow and slow running, but they did generate enough energy to run a few gristmills in the early centuries of settlement and development.

The town, along with Tiverton to the north, is part of the mainland, politically separated from the rest of the state by Massachusetts, of which the town was a part until 1747. Little Compton's isolation has been key, at times a self-reinforcing factor in the town's development throughout its history.

The area named Little Compton was the domain of the Sakonnets, a subtribe of the Wampanoag nation. The tribe's leader, Queen Awashonks, befriended the white settlers. An inscription on a rock in Wilbour Woods commemorates this friendship as "Awashonks, friend of the Whiteman." Because of Awashonks's friendship, the tribe sided with Captain Church, greatly aiding him in the victory that ended King Philip's War.

Captain Benjamin Church and thirty others who followed him from Duxbury and Marshfield established the settlement in 1673. In 1675, Church built his homestead in Little Compton, just before King Philip's War. Today, a plaque on the side of West Main Road gives the location of his original homestead. Some to whom land was granted include Governor Winslow and William Pabodie, who had married Betty Alden, the daughter of Pricilla and John Alden.

In 1682, the Plymouth Colony incorporated the village, officially naming it Little Compton. This is possibly a reference to Little Compton in Warwickshire, England. By 1747, Little Compton had secured its own royal decree, joining Newport County as a part of the colony of Rhode Island along with Tiverton and Bristol. Because Little Compton was once part of the Plymouth Colony, all probate and land records before 1746 are in Taunton and New Bedford, Massachusetts archives.

During the Revolution, inhabitants were hardly disturbed. They did their part in helping the cause of independence by establishing an outpost from which to spy on the British occupying Aquidneck Island. Isaac Barker of Middletown kept an eye on British movements on the island. Whenever any proposed movement of British troops came to Barker's attention, he concealed a letter describing the intelligence under a certain rock on the shore and at the same time placing a signal light in a particular position on high ground near the hidden message. During the night, Little Compton Patriots crossed the Sakonnet River, retrieved the message and rushed it to the commander of colonial forces.

Otherwise, as war and peace alternately prevailed throughout the country, Little Compton had little interest in foreign intrigues except when men were enlisted to serve in distant parts.

A LITTLE COMPTON TOUR

The extreme southern part of the area, now in Rhode Island and situated between the Massachusetts boundary and the Sakonnet River below the township of Tiverton, is Little Compton. This place contains a great deal of rolling, rocky upland; a swampy and much-indented seacoast with many hidden coves; a coastline much loved during prohibition by smugglers in small, swift inboard speedboats; some old farmland and fishing settlements; and many old homesteads—all settled in three principal villages.

S'connet Point is located at the extreme southwestern tip of the town. It had a cluster of fishing shanties, small cottages and modest summer retreats of the wealthy.

Adamsville is a small village at the head of a deep coastal estuary extending a considerable distance inland from the ocean to the south, with a collection of old and new houses grouped about the old Manchester and Gray Stores in the northeastern corner of the town, hard up against the Massachusetts line.

Little Compton Commons is another small settlement, located almost in the geographical center of the area; here also is a mixture of antique and recently constructed dwellings.

Otherwise, the township contains much unoccupied fallow land, many Indian sites and burial grounds, a large number of summer cottages—especially along its eastern coastline—and a surprisingly large number of old homesteads, principally aligned along the main north and south roads, extending up to Tiverton and Fall River at the north. In 1790, it is recorded the town population numbered 1,542 whites and 23 slaves.

Ebenezer P. Church built the old Manchester Store (destroyed by fire in 2002) in 1820, and until it was converted to a restaurant in the mid-1950s, it continued operation as a general merchandise emporium, with many of the original fixtures and little concession to modern ideas about the display of goods. The store came into the possession of Philip Manchester in 1839, and from that time, a member of the Manchester family has always run it.

One of the most eye-catching houses in the local group is a large white structure, overshadowed by huge trees one hundred feet or more in height and located almost on the Massachusetts line, a few hundred feet to the east of the store. This attractive structure dates from about 1818–25, and the two other small, appealing houses are found nearby, across the street to the west of the store and down the side street leading to Westport.

From this small, quiet village, the principal east–west road climbs steeply up a hill, goes past a little stone cottage and, after many turns and twists, passes another small shrub-covered cottage and then enters Little Compton Commons, a somewhat larger group of houses located nearly halfway to the shores of the Sakonnet River. Here is located the small but attractive Brownell Cottage, with its unusual divided interior stairway.

A mile or so north of Little Compton's upper boundary, near the southern edge of Tiverton, is Tiverton Four Corners—an intersection of the main north–south roadway, with a cross road that continues to the east and south into Little Compton territory at Adamsville, where it passes into Massachusetts almost as quickly.

Only a few hundred yards beyond this intersection to the south is the old Peregrine White gristmill, where residents brought their grain for grinding into Rhode Island Jonny Cake Meal. According to a sign on the mill's front façade, meal is ground two days each week. Still within a half mile distance are one of the stores and no fewer than four of the old houses built by members of the White family, several of which still house descendants of the White family; the White Homestead is a little south of the mill. Members of the White family were well-known mariners on whaling vessels sailing out of New Bedford. The White family's burying ground is located on this farm and contains, among others, a stone in memory of the child of Peregrine White of the ship *Mayflower*. The old headstones were removed to the Amicable Churchyard nearby. We assume that the remains of the departed still rest in their original internment place.

Turning west, across a saltwater inlet onto Puncatest Neck, is the Colonel Cooke House, shown as a landmark on a map dated 1730; the house has retained a charming and unique old doorway.

Following on south along this same highway, one passes other old houses overlooking the Sakonnet River and Aquidneck Island to the west. Nearly all of the other dwellings mentioned in this narrative are located here, including the Oliver H. Almy House and the house of Captain Robert

Gray, who discovered the Columbia River and was the first American to carry the Stars and Stripes around the world. Another historic house is the Betty Alden House. William Pabodie built the east portion for him and his wife, Elizabeth Alden, in 1682. They were among the first settlers, and their descendants occupied the house until it came into the possession of Colonel Pardon Gray in 1762. That is when the western ell was added. Nearby is the 1691 home of Samuel and Mary (Potter) Wilbor, two other original settlers.

The main highway continues out to the extreme end of the peninsula, to the lighthouse at S'connet Point. Passing along the way, visitors can see other early houses and cottages, as well as many newer summer dwellings, particularly in the southwestern portion of the town overlooking the shores and beaches along the lower Sakonnet River and the Atlantic Ocean.

WILBOR HOUSE

The following was written by the Little Compton Historical Society.

Wilbor House, the Little Compton Historical Society's headquarters, stands on land purchased from the Sakonnet Indians in 1673. Built by Samuel Wilbor in about 1680, the original house consisted of only two rooms,

Wilbor House, headquarters of the Little Compton Historical Society. *Courtesy of the Little Compton Historical Society.*

The fully restored Wilbor House living room, furnished in authentic eighteenth-century style. *Courtesy of the Little Compton Historical Society.*

one above the other, and a cramped stairway and attic. It was typical of seventeenth-century New England.

Today, one unusual feature of Wilbor House is that it spans four centuries and contains rooms that are representative of each. Eight generations of Wilbors (variously spelled Wilbore, Wilbor, Willbour, Wilber and Wilbur) continuously occupied it until after 1900.

The Little Compton Historical Society incorporated in 1937 to preserve landmarks and to identify historical sites in the town. The society also assembles, acquires and preserves books, documents, photographs and other material relating to the history of Little Compton.

Town Churches and Public Schools

There are only a few seventeenth-century structures still standing, including the Wilbor and Peabody Houses, which date from the eighteenth and nineteenth centuries. The Quaker meetinghouse on West Main Road, No. 8 Schoolhouse (now used as part of the town hall), Wilbur's Store and the United Congregational Church—all predating 1900—center on the Commons. Additional historic homes are scattered throughout the town and include the Asa Gray House, the Slicer House, Oldacre, the Brownell House on West Main Road, the Brownell House on Meetinghouse Lane, the William Whalley Homestead on Burchard Avenue (on the National Register of Historic Places) and the Brownell Library on the Commons.

Church and State

In the period following King Philip's War, the town drew more settlers, remaining a quiet, rural town primarily composed of agricultural and fishing interests. The settlers from Plymouth Colony were mainly Congregationalists. The town meetinghouse built on the Commons in 1693 was both a Congregational meetinghouse and a town hall. To the Plymouth Puritans, church and state were linked.

Independently minded and acting contrary to the mandates from the Plymouth General Court, Little Compton did not immediately establish an official Congregational church edifice or parish house. Despite setting aside ample land for use and support of a preacher, it was not until 1701 that a Congregational minister was in continuous residence in the town. The fledgling community with a small population could ill afford supporting a minister, and perhaps such an assignment held little appeal for a missionary minister.

Throughout the 1680s, the town did not pay the ministerial tax levied by the Plymouth General Court, and in 1686, the court therefore fined the town twenty pounds for "contempt and neglect." Further, by 1700 a sufficient number of Quakers who had no interest in supporting a Congregational church resided in the town and had built their Quaker meetinghouse, the first strictly religious structure in the town. It was located on West Main Road on the site of the present Quaker meetinghouse.

The mixing of Congregational and Quaker sects certainly indicates a liberal attitude toward religious tolerance and more closely aligns Little Compton to the religious open-mindedness and separation of church and state in nearby Rhode Island Colony than to Plymouth Colony.

A THUMBNAIL SKETCH OF TOWN CHURCHES

The following monograph, by B.R. Jacobakind, first appeared in the 1975 Little Compton Tercentennial yearbook.

The Churches of Little Compton all share one common tradition: they all began with visiting ministry holding services in private homes or public buildings. The first religious teacher, chosen by public town meeting September 7, 1698, was Eliphalet Adams, and the first building used exclusively for religious worship was the Friends meeting house, 1700.

There have been seven different religious faiths officially established over the years in Little Compton. The oldest and best documented historically is The United Congregational Church, also known as the "White Church," as it was known before 1846. In the 17th and 18th centuries, the Quakers and the Congregationalists were alone in their worship. The 19th century saw the establishment of the Methodists, led by Lemuel Sisson who founded their meetinghouse in 1825, the Mormons, founded by missionaries for the Reorganized Church of Jesus Christ of Latter Day Saints from New Bedford, the Christian Baptists (a sect which no longer worships in Little Compton), an offshoot of the Tiverton Baptist Church (The Old Stone Church), and the organization of the Roman Catholics. Shortly after the turn of the 20th century the Roman Catholics erected their first church (1910) and were followed by the Episcopalians [whose] Mission Chapel of St. Andrew-by-the-Sea (1914) serves today as a summer chapel. The 20th century also saw the union (1940) of the Methodists and the Congregationalists in the present United Congregational Church building.

It is interesting to note that Little Compton was a frontrunner of the concept of separation of church and state, for by 1787 the town had established a policy of leaving all church affairs in the hands of the individual church and its society.

THE CONGREGATIONAL CHURCH

The United Congregational Church edifice was erected in 1832; additional construction and renovations took place in 1871, 1974 and 1986. It is a white clapboard building, three bays deep and set on a high basement foundation, with a projecting central pavilion, tower and spire. Built originally as an austere meetinghouse, the building was raised and remodeled in 1871; Gothic details added to the tower and spire date from that period.

The Congregational Church has always been an important institution in Little Compton. The act of incorporation provided for "a right of land granted to the exclusive use of the ministry." Disregarding the concept of separation of church and state, the minister was chosen by a vote of the electors at a town meeting. Because the "elected" minister was in residence in Massachusetts, no municipal tax was levied for his support, as was the practice in Rhode Island. Without a church edifice for a period of twenty-five years, services were held in the town meetinghouse.

The second building, first occupied in 1724, stood in about the same location as the current edifice. By the early 1830s, this building was dilapidated, so the Congregational Society voted to replace it in March 1832. Adjacent to the church is the Commons burying ground, and together they present a Currier and Ives image of a New England village.

The Methodist Church

The original two-story 1842 Greek Revival structure with a three-bay façade and pediment end-gable roof above a broad entablature is now altered. Formerly, the building had a short tower centered above the façade, paired entrances in the end bays and broad steps in the full width of the building. Little Compton's earliest Methodist services were held in Lemuel Sisson's house at S'connet Point; the first Methodist church erected, in 1825, was located on West Main Road. This building was superseded by a later structure erected just across the street at the west end of the

Thrifty citizens recycle their public buildings for many uses. This building, built in 1840 and seen in November 1996, was the original Methodist church, later serving as the Odd Fellows Hall in 1872. It now sees use as the police department headquarters.

The Methodist church served Little Compton for many decades from this spot on the Commons. After consolidation with the Congregational Church, the old Methodist church edifice was torn down.

Commons in 1872, after which this building was converted to use as a lodge by Independent Order of Odd Fellows. The later Methodist church, severely damaged by the 1944 hurricane, was demolished. By that time, Methodists had joined the Congregationalists in worship.

THE QUAKERS

George Fox, son of an English weaver, is the founder of the Quakers, and he began preaching in 1648. Shortly afterward, many became followers, and by the year 1655, about seventy-five were preaching the Quaker doctrine whenever and wherever they could find an audience. The early doctrine of the Quakers is difficult to describe because the sect had no written creed or articles of religious worship.

Evidently, they believed that the best form of worship was the patient waiting on God in silence. Their views underwent many changes with the passage of time, but it was not their religious point of view, their creed or the absence of creed that frequently led to persecution. Rather, it was their manners. Quakers adopted a simple salutation in addressing an individual, however dignified, as the "thee" and "thou" used for a magistrate or a judge.

They refused to bow or remove their hats, often the cause for great irritation. They refused to say "good morning," "good day" or "good night," and they used numbers instead of names for the months of the year and the days of the week. For these reasons, Quakers suffered.

Quakers adopted a remarkable simplicity in their marriages and their funerals; their houses, furniture and form of dress were extremely plain. Both men and women were easily identified as Quakers by their simple attire. They wore no symbols of mourning after the death of a relative. Otherwise, Quakers believed in the common doctrines of Christianity, especially that the scriptures proceeded from the spirit of God. Their simplicity, refusal to adhere to common customs, independence and opposition toward rules and regulations accepted willingly by the public brought severe persecution upon them.

The first Quakers arrived in Boston in 1656 and soon became the objects of special Massachusetts legislation. Imprisonment, fines, branding, mutilation, banishment and death were the results of the bigotry against these sincere Christians.

Conversely, Rhode Island had the reputation of tolerance for persons with "different" religious beliefs; the colony became a refuge for such persecuted people. The commissioners of the United Colonies, perceiving this, wrote to Rhode Island in 1657, asking it to banish the Quakers already there and then prohibit any more arrivals. The Rhode Island General Assembly answered, "We have no law among us whereby to punish any, for only declaring the words in their minds concerning the things and ways of God." Thus, Rhode Island steadfastly adhered to its principles of toleration.

The result of Quaker persecution outside Rhode Island, and the acceptance of those followers within, was the attainment of great wealth and political influence by Quakers on both sides of Narragansett Bay. Quakers in Little Compton formed a meeting in 1700, assisted by Friends in Dartmouth and Portsmouth. Portions of the original meetinghouse built in 1815 were incorporated in the new structure on the current site on West Main Road.

The last Little Compton Quaker died in 1903, and the meetinghouse became dilapidated. In 1947, the Westport Monthly Meeting of Quakers gave the building to the Little Compton Historical Society, which fully restored it in 1960. The form of this serenely simple building reflects the ideals of the Friends' worship. The two entrances and the divisibility of the interior accommodate the segregation of sexes during meeting.

The Quaker meetinghouse, owned and restored by the Little Compton Historical Society. *Courtesy of the Little Compton Historical Society.*

At a time when the Friends' strength was waning, this is the only nineteenth-century Quaker meetinghouse built in rural Rhode Island. That Little Compton Quakers elected to build a new meetinghouse at this time suggests that the movement was still vigorous.

GETTING AN EDUCATION

In February 1800, the Rhode Island legislature established a free school system throughout the state. Each community in the state appropriated money for the operation of the free schools. The length of the school session appears to not have been legislated because Little Compton maintained three schools for four months each year. Only white children between the ages of six and twenty years attended the classes in reading, writing and common arithmetic.

Beginning in 1828, the state began chipping in for support of the schools. In 1860, the state appropriated $745 to Little Compton, and the town added $300 to support the eight schools with an enrollment of 277.

The following account of the seven district schools appeared in the April 1870 issue of the *Little Compton Platonic* newspaper. The research and collection of the descriptions of the schools reproduced here was done by Doris E. Simmons. Her narrative appeared in the 1975 Little Compton Tercentennial yearbook:

DISTRICT NO. 1

A good degree of interest was manifested in this school among the pupils, owing to the enthusiasm of their teacher in his profession. A reward was offered by the teacher, and also Col. Henry T. Sisson, the trustee, to the one who should make the greatest progress in writing and in spelling, which greatly stimulated the scholars, and promoted their interest in their studies. The school deserves the approbation of the Committee and employers. Length of term, 77 days; whole number registered 18; average attendance, 17.

DISTRICT NO. 2

This school, under the care of Mrs. Deborah Gray, was considered by the portion of the employers [parents], *as nearly a failure. Mrs. Gray entered the school under unfavorable circumstances, the impression existing that her qualifications were not equal to the requirements of the school. Though she labored diligently, and we believe faithfully, she was not able, wholly to change that impression; yet we think she gave satisfaction to a majority of her employment. Length of term, four months, whole number registered 11; average attendance 7, or nearly 64 per cent of the number registered. The trustee did not visit the school.*

DISTRICT NO. 3

This school was taught by Mrs. Mary S. Gray, who labored with fair results for the improvement of her pupils. Length of school term four months; whole number registered, 17, average attendance, 14, or 82 percent of the number registered. Not visited by the trustee.

DISTRICT NO. 7

This school was taught by Miss. Ammie E. Field, and her labors were measurably successful. Could Miss. Field attend a Normal School for one or two terms, her efforts would be much more successful. Length of term, four months, whole number registered 22, average attendance, 15, or 68 per cent of the number registered. One visit from the trustee.

DISTRICT NO. 8
This school, under the care and instruction of Miss. Helen A. Tompkins, made a commendable progress, and general satisfaction was given. Length of term, five months; whole number registered 26; average attendance, 18, or 69 per cent of the number registered. Not visited by the trustee.

DISTRICT NO. 9
Miss. Hattie M. Taylor, teacher. It was her first attempt at teaching and though lacking somewhat in method and perhaps in decision, she labored diligently for the improvement of her pupils, and with a fair degree of success. Length of term, four months; whole number registered, 12; average attendance, 9, or 75 per cent of the number registered. One visit from the trustee.

DISTRICT NO. 10
In this school, Miss. Abbie M. Shaw fully sustained her reputation as a teacher. Mild in government, sometimes, perhaps, to the detriment of the school, she had the faculty of interesting her pupils. Her method of teaching arithmetic was excellent, and the progress of her pupils in that branch was specially apparent; and though glad that as Mrs. Bailey, she has a changing her name, found more agreeable occupation, we regret the loss our schools will thereby sustain. Length of term, four and one-half months; whole number registered, 17, average attendance, 12, or 70 per cent of the number registered. The trustee twice visited this school.

No account is given of Districts 4, 5 and six at this time.

In 1885 there were ten school districts, each having a summer and winter term. The summer term started in April or May, and the winter term in November or December. Total number of school days was about 160. The smallest number of pupils enrolled in a school was 9 and the largest 32, but the average daily attendance for from seven to 20.

Teachers' pay ranged from $25 to $27 per month. There were 12 women teachers and three men. Some taught only one term or less.

In a financial town meeting as early as 1879, F.R. Brownell was elected a member of the School Committee for three years, and A.M. Rice *was elected Superintendent of Schools. A proposition to reduce the salary of Superintendent of Schools from $40 to $25 was voted down, though the Superintendent elect consented to a reduction, the former sum being considered quite little enough to secure a faithful discharge of the office.*

The report of the Superintendent of Schools was read and accepted, and the sum of $1500 was voted for the use of public schools for the ensuing year.

In 1885 a provision was made at the May session of the State Legislature making it optional for the town to change from the district to the town system, whereby the control of the public schools was vested in the school committee of five members.

Captain Benjamin Church

Benjamin Church was born in Duxbury, Massachusetts, in 1639. His father, a carpenter by trade, was one of Governor Winthrop's band of settlers. For a while, young Benjamin followed his father's trade with some success in Duxbury. In May 1670, Church, a freeman, was sworn as a constable of the town. In 1674, a few years after his marriage to Alice Southworth, he learned of land available in Plymouth Colony's Sakonnet lands. Here, he established a homestead and farm near the East Passage of the Sakonnet River; Church, his wife and a small band of followers were the first Englishmen to settle in that territory.

The youthful settler had little chance to develop his farm. When the threat of Indian warfare began to rapidly escalate, Church was summoned by Plymouth Colony. He was especially well fitted to be a great Indian fighter. In stature, he is described as "tall and well proportioned, and his frame well knit, built for activity and endurance. As a young man, he was exceedingly active and vigorous, characteristics, which strongly recommended him to his Indian neighbors. In his residence of a year among the Indians, he gained a thorough knowledge of their character and acquired a great influence among them." With his great religious convictions and desire for glory, he was fully prepared to aid the Plymouth colonists.

During his residence among the Sakonnet Indians, he often attended their celebratory feasts and their war dances. Here, he found the female sachem Awashonks leading the rites. Armed delegates from the Mount

Hope Pokanoket Wampanoag tribe were also there, and more than once Church's life hung in the balance as the "dance-maddened" braves regarded him with hostile eyes.

Paying no attention to the dangers of his own situation, Church argued long and earnestly with Awashonks, finally persuading her to submit to the Plymouth Colony. Later, on his journey back to Plymouth, he met Weetamoe, queen sachem of the Pocasset tribe, and won her allegiance as well. However, despite his efforts, war was started by Wampanoag sachem Metacom,[19] and the Pocassets were drawn into the conflict against Plymouth.

In his 1958 book *Flintlock and Tomahawk*, author Douglas Edward Leach gave a detailed account of Church's meeting with Awashonks:

> *Also about the middle of June, Awashonks held a dance to which she invited Benjamin Church, the pioneer settler in the Sakonnet country. Church, who at this time was a vigorous and aggressive man in his mid-thirties, had established a farm in what is now Little Compton, and had managed to win the friendship and respect of the neighboring female sachem* [Awashonks]. *At the dance Church found not only a large number of Sakonnets, but also six of Philip's own Indians, their faces smeared with war paint. It soon became clear that these six were there for persuading the Sakonnets to join Philip in resisting the English. After hearing their arguments, Awashonks turned to her friend Church, and while the six painted Wampanoags glowered fiercely at him, he boldly urged the wavering female sachem to remain loyal to the Plymouth government. Seemingly successful in his appeal, Church left the Sakonnets and headed for the Pocasset country and Plymouth. En route, he talked with Peter Nunnuit, the husband of Weetamoe, who gave him to understand that Philip was actually bent on war, and that other Indians were even now flocking in to his support. Early on the morning of June 16, Church hastened into the presence of Governor Winslow, and related his experiences of the past few days. Added to what the authorities already suspected, this report was grim news indeed.*

Throughout the weary months of fighting, in which the Indians were at first successful, Church served as a leader of the United Colonial Militia. Many times, his troops disregarded his wise counsel. Regardless, Church remained steadfast, using his keen knowledge of the ways of Indian warfare in the English cause.

During the early months of the war, the Indians spread fire and death all over New England. More than six hundred of the best English fighting men were killed, and many settlements were put to the torch. Nevertheless, the tide of events gradually turned, and the Indians began to suffer defeats that broke up their determination and scattered their warriors.

Canonchet, son of Monatomi, entered the war with hope of avenging his father's death but was killed himself. In the battle at Bridgewater Swamp, Philip's hopes of ever driving the English from his land were shattered. The final betrayal of Philip came when bands of Indians gradually went over to the English side.

When the number of Weetamoe's fighting men was reduced from three hundred to only twenty-six, they were driven to a swamp in Swansea. While trying to escape by night, Weetamoe passed on to Mount Hope Bay, which she attempted to cross on a raft, drowning in the process.

THE BATTLE OF ALMY'S "PEASEFIELD"

A vaguely defined area between Neck Road and the Sakonnet River just north of Fogland Road was the scene of one of the first engagements in King Philip's War of 1675–76.

On June 30, 1675, King Philip crossed from Mount Hope to Tiverton with six hundred men, and for eighteen days, they held off an English attack by a force led by Church. Church dogged Philip from the Stone Bridge area southward toward S'connet Point. Church's company discovered tracks of Wampanoag braves, but when attempting to follow them, they were met with a massive volley of gunfire from a force twenty times larger than Church's. After this, retreat and regrouping became the plan.

In July 1675, Captains Matthew Fuller and Benjamin Church, with a troop of about forty men, crossed the Sakonnet River into Pocasset territory in an attempt to capture the unsuspecting Philip. Fuller and Church split into groups of about twenty men each. When Fuller's group met with Wampanoag warriors, they retreated and ferried back to Aquidneck Island.

Church's men were pinned down in John Almy's abandoned peasefield along the Sakonnet shore. After six hours of strategic retreat and holding off the Indians, Captain Goulding aboard his sloop floated a canoe to the shore, extricating Church and his men, two at a time, from their predicament.[20]

Eventually, Church won the aid of Awashonks; 140 of her braves were enlisted to fight against Philip. The capture of Philip's war chief Annawon was a severe blow against his forces; however, Philip's fearlessness and calculating courage made him extremely feared by his people.

In the final blow to end the war, Church led his English troops and Indian allies into the swamp at Mount Hope, surrounding the Wampanoag chief in a net from which he could not escape.

FIGHTING DAYS ENDED

Church's devotion to Plymouth Colony during the war was marred by constant disagreements and petty jealousies among the English leaders. The chastening power of their repeated defeats at the hands of the Indian foe made his opponents eventually give him the command he should have had from the beginning of the conflict.

The ruins of Captain Church's Bristol homestead are seen in this circa 1840 photo.

At the beginning of the war, Church evacuated his family from his Sakonnet homestead and sent them into Rhode Island's Mount Hope Neck for safety. At war's end in 1676, the place (soon to become the town of Bristol) was a small, unincorporated seaside village. Here Church settled down, building a house on the north side of Constitution Street, near Thames Street. The last remnant of the old homestead is long gone; a stone slab with a bronze plaque commemorates the spot.

At the apex of his popularity, the people of the village, honoring the conqueror of Philip, elected Captain Church to many town offices, thereby ensuring the fulfillment of these responsibilities with dispatch and honesty.

As an honored and respected elector of the village, he signed and sealed the "Grand Articles" for the settlement of the Mount Hope Neck and Poppasquash Neck on September 14, 1680. On July 7, 1681, the Plymouth General Court authorized Church to "cutt and cleare" a more direct way from Mount Hope to Boston. The first proprietors of Mount Hope, seventy-six in number and with Captain Benjamin Church heading the list, decided that the name of the new town should be Bristol while meeting in concert on September 1, 1681.

Church's accolades continued, with added honors and responsibilities. In May 1682, he was chosen deputy to represent Bristol at the Colonial Court, at which time he was also chosen first selectman of the town, positions he held during his residence at Bristol. In July 1682, he was commissioned a magistrate authorized to solemnize marriages. He was one of the original eight members of the First Congregational Church of Bristol.

Much to his disappointment, his days of fighting were to continue. In 1689, the French and Indians were aggressors and Maine the seat of conflict. Church was given the rank of major and commander-in-chief and headed an expedition into Maine, but he was hampered by a lack of support from the colonial governments. Massachusetts had little interest in the welfare of its neighboring colony. Church was called back to report the conditions in Maine to the Massachusetts authorities. He was again sent northward with a force of 250 men. Again, Massachusetts withdrew its support after the men were in the field, and Church, thoroughly disgusted, disbanded his company.

At age sixty-five Church retired from military life. In 1696 or 1697, he traveled to Fall River with his brother Caleb, purchased land, erected a sawmill and a gristmill and improved the waterpower. He sold his share of the enterprise in September 1714 to Richard Borden of Tiverton and Joseph Borden of Fall River.

Captain Benjamin Church (circa 1639–1718) in an 1864 wood engraved print from a disbound copy of *Indian Races of North and South America*. A carpenter by trade, he was a military officer and Ranger during the American colonial era.

He continued living with his family in Bristol until 1705, when he returned to his original homestead farm in Little Compton. Fortunately, his vigor in times of peace as well as in war gave him the means to acquire enough real estate, including mills and water privileges in Bristol, Fall River, Tiverton and Little Compton, to avoid any poverty during his old age.

Thrown from his horse while returning from a visit to his sister on January 16, 1718, he was severely injured, precipitating his death about twelve hours afterward. His burial at the Little Compton Commons Cemetery was accompanied with great pomp and military honors.

AROUND THE COMMONS

Villages arise around a focal point, such as common ground, a public building, a mill, a store, a port or harbor, a post office or a crossroad. As a remote town, beyond well-traveled roads or sea lanes, and as a town with negligible industrial potential, Little Compton developed only two actual villages, the Commons and Adamsville. At an early date, another settlement, now gone, existed at S'connet Point.

As recorded in three past federal censes reports, the permanent population of Little Compton has remained constant: 3,367 in 1980, 3,593 in 2000 and 3,492 in 2010.

Little Compton is the location for one of two town commons in Rhode Island. The other is in Bristol. This is most likely a result of the town's original layout by settlers from the Plymouth and Massachusetts Colonies. In August 1677, land designated for the common was selected and has been used ever since as both a religious and civic center for social activities in the town.

The creation of a combined civic and religious focus, completely at odds with Rhode Island settlements of the seventeenth century, was common in the Plymouth and Massachusetts Bay Colonies. The establishment of the Commons in 1677—three years after the first land division—probably reflects the instability of the town's first years during King Philip's War, as well as the proprietors' desire to proceed with the town's settlement. The proprietors selected the Commons' location by vote: "[A]ll the proprietors shall go thither to view and give their judgments concerning the premises."

The Commons' location on a hillock above marshes and streams is of irregular shape and lacks a strict cardinal alignment, which implies an organic, topographical orientation. The nucleus is the Commons' land located near the geographical center of the town, with a meetinghouse, small house lots and a burial ground. The creation of house lots around the Commons suggests that settlement may have occurred there as well. The variance among early lot sizes suggests the presence of houses around the Commons, with outlying fields as well as discrete outlying farmsteads.

The seventeenth-century Commons was centrally located; it has remained the preeminent village within the town since its creation. Its civic role was intensified as new buildings were erected around its periphery throughout the nineteenth century. The Methodist church, stores, blacksmiths' shops and civic buildings supplemented the meetinghouse and the Congregational Church. The town's first post office was opened for business in 1804 at Adamsville, and a second post office was opened at the Commons in 1834.

During these formative years, the Commons began to experience institutional growth that reinforced its importance: the Methodist church (1840), with a larger, successor structure (1872); the No. 8 School (circa 1845); and the Union Cemetery (1850). The only institution not here was the Friends Meetinghouse, which has always existed on West Main Road because most of its members lived in that part of town.

By the early 1860s, the Commons boasted a building boom. In addition to the Congregational and Methodist churches, the post office, the school, town hall and two cemeteries, new additions included three dry goods stores, two smithies, a shoe shop and twenty residences. In the late nineteenth and early twentieth centuries, the Commons saw the addition of a new town hall (1880), the grange hall (1902), the Brownell Library (1929), the Josephine Wilbour School (1920) and several new houses.

No. 8 Schoolhouse, circa 1845, is a one-story clapboard building set gable end to the street with a bracket, hip-roof cupola set above the three-bay façade, which has a pair of narrow six-over-six sash windows in the center. The building continued to serve as a school until completion of the Wilbour School in 1929. In 1986–87, it was connected to the town hall by an addition at the rear of the building.

The Little Compton Town Hall began service in April 1882. The original town hall, built on the Commons in 1693, served both civic and religious gatherings; the old structure stood until 1917, when it burned down.

The old Grange Hall, seen here in November 1996, served the community in many capacities: Little Compton Grange No. 32, the No. 8 Public School and the town hall.

THE GRANGE HALL, a shingled two-and-a-half-story structure built in 1902, housed the Little Compton Grange No. 32, which was established in 1894 with forty-nine charter members. The Grange movement began in the American Midwest in the 1860s as a strong political force; in New England, it was a social and educational institution. The movement came to Rhode Island in 1887.

THE BROWNELL LIBRARY, circa 1929, began as a private library established under the will of Pardon C. Brownell (1841–1921). It operated as a free library for the citizens of Little Compton until in 1961, when the Brownell Library merged with the town's Free Public Library, established in 1879, with facilities housed in the town hall. Following the merger, the public library moved into the Brownell building, expanded in 1961–63 to accommodate both collections.

ABRAM WORDELL'S BLACKSMITH SHOP is the only remaining of two smithy shops built at the Commons in the nineteenth century. Blacksmiths played important roles in nineteenth-century agricultural society; their tasks included shoeing horses, making and mending farm tools and domestic homestead items and manufacturing and repairing wagon parts. Wordell's building, now somewhat altered, still recalls a significant activity in the town center.

HISTORIC CEMETERIES

There are about fifty-seven historic cemeteries in the town. Colonel Benjamin Church and his family are buried at the Little Compton Commons Cemetery, as is Elizabeth Alden Pabodie, the eldest daughter of John Alden and Priscilla Mullins of *Mayflower* fame, who is alleged to have been the first white woman born in New England. She died at age ninety-four on May 31, 1717. The stones in the cemetery reflect a style of carving similar to that found both in Newport and in Boston during the same period.

The old Burying Ground (1675) at the Commons is located immediately west of the Congregational Church, with north–south rows of headstones. The earliest of these date from the seventeenth century, and the cemetery includes a number of slate markers, both vertical and ledger stones. This is the final resting place for the remains of several figures prominent in local history.

The Union Cemetery (1850) is a small private cemetery on the south side of the Commons and has many granite and marble stones dating from the mid- to late nineteenth century. Notable markers include a statue of Colonel Henry T. Sisson and the town's Civil War commemorative monument.

ADAMSVILLE AND SPITE TOWER

Politically, the village of Adamsville is part of Little Compton. Geographically, it is part of three towns and two states: Little Compton and Tiverton in Rhode Island and Westport in Massachusetts. Socially, it is a place where everyone seems to know everybody else. When residents visit town hall, a library or any of the small local businesses, they are greeted by name.

The flinty spirit of early colonials is alive here. Things get done quickly, efficiently and without fuss. The true old Yankee virtues of thrift and frugality are alive and well in Adamsville. The connection to colonial America is in ample evidence in the town's carefully preserved historic architecture. Adamsville, settled by a Baptist community, has always been the part of the town where the "common folk" live. The Old Stone Baptist Church, in Tiverton, was the Adamsville congregation's house of worship, as well as the site for many years of an annual clambake that was an important social event in the area.

Adamsville is a hamlet, and it is just far enough away from the Commons to have its own personality, general store and post office. Most people on this side of Little Compton thought that Adamsville was a little more isolated than the rest of the town.

Little Compton's coastal location and unspoiled beauty has brought a large number of summer residents; anyone who loves New England and its seasons could not fail to be charmed by the bare trees and stark and beautiful landscape of this town in late fall.

Nobody comes through Adamsville accidentally, as the hamlet is a remote peninsula. For many years, the place was ignored. People did not care to visit since it was just too far out of the way. In a December 3, 2006 *Providence Journal* article, eighty-nine-year-old Carlton Brownell, Little Compton's unofficial town historian said, "Our business is the summer people. Summer residents are mostly people who like quiet. They don't want to go to Newport; some have built hideous places."

THE SPITE TOWER

Only in a rural setting like Little Compton could a three-story, forty-five-foot tower claim skyscraper status. The story behind this odd circa 1905 building is an intriguing one, owning something to both fact and legend.

When Abraham Manchester's father died, he took over management of the Adamsville store.[21] His sisters, Deborah and Elizabeth, lived in the family home diagonally across the street; Abraham had his bedroom above the store. When he wished to send a simple signal to his sisters at home, he did so by waving a cloth out the store's second-floor window. At this late date, we can only conjecture how well this system worked.

Here is where legend takes over and blurs factual history. A certain Dr. John Hathaway took up residence with his wife, Claudia, in the former Samuel Church House[22] on the property between the store and the Manchester home. Legend has it that the doctor had a romantic interest in one of the Manchester sisters. When his interest was unrequited, he had the tower built at just the right point to block the formerly unobstructed view between the Manchester home and the store, thus frustrating communication from brother to sisters.

Dr. Hathaway's intentions regarding the tower may have been pure. Perhaps he simply wanted to ensure an ample supply of water for his household. The structure, built over a well, serves as a wellhead, with the pump on the first floor, the tank on the third and living quarters on the second.

Whatever the fact in the matter, the legend makes a good story, and it earned Dr. Hathaway's unusual well house an appropriately colorful name: the Spite Tower.

GRAY'S GENERAL STORE

According to Grayton Waite, owner and proprietor of Gray's General Store, the shop is the oldest continually operating store in the state and possibly the country, built in 1788 by Samuel Church. The store looks pretty much the same as it did when it was first opened for business. Gray's is as much a museum as it is a store. It appears that no piece of store fixture was ever thrown away.

Once you enter the country store, you see the remains of Little Compton's first post office, still maintained after being closed for about eighty years. The loafing room is still there, where old-time village gents would gather to hang out and discuss news of the day. The loafing room features a bench that was kept very warm in the old days. Grayton noted that his grandpa used to say that old guys who had nothing to do just came in here to stay from six o'clock in the morning until eight o'clock at night—you might say it was an old boy's clubhouse.

The store is situated near the banks of the Acoaxet River. Right behind it is the old gristmill, where farmers still grind corn into jonnycake meal, which Gray's sells. Built in 1675, it is the country's oldest continuously

A circa 1938 photo of the Adamsville Philip L. Gray general store. *Courtesy of Millicent A. Waite.*

operated mill. John Hart, Grayton's grandfather, ran the mill for more than sixty years.

Grayton, about fifty years old, burly and a graphic designer, is the sixth generation of his family to run the store. His great-great-grandfather, Philip L. Gray, purchased the store from the estate of Samuel Church in 1879, and it has remained in the family since. Grayton's grandmother, Marion Gray Hart, became postmistress in 1919. When Marion gave birth to Millicent in 1927, her brother, Herman J. Gray, took over as postmaster. The job did not last long because 1927 was the year the government closed the post office.

The store's longevity is enhanced by Grayton's admirable passion for preserving the Adamsville landmark, making it a warm place for people to come enjoy a slice of early Americana. Gray's still sells the classics like penny candy and soda pop, jonnycake meal, cigars and locally made cheese. Not every visitor is a history buff; some make the trip to Adamsville out of curiosity. Uniquely, the village has managed to preserve the quintessential New England charm that so many other towns have lost during the years for the sake of modernizing.

RHODE ISLAND RED MONUMENT (1925)

In Adamsville, there is a large granite boulder with a bronze tablet bearing the image of a chicken with the inscription: "To commemorate the birthplace of the breed of Rhode Island fowl which originated near this location." The breed indeed originated at William Tripps's farm on Long Highway. The marker is placed just across the street near the Manchester Store because many of these birds were sold at that store.

Development of the Rhode Island red breed of chicken is credited to William Tripp, John Macomber and Isaac C. Wilbour. In the 1850s, Tripp and Macomber began experimenting with crossbreeding Asian red cocks with native hens.[23] Wilbour crossbred his own stock of Plymouth Rock hens with the Asian reds; the offspring of this experiment became known locally as Tripp fowls. The bird, developed in the early 1890s and known as the Rhode Island red, proved to be a great improvement over previous commercial fowl because it laid more and larger eggs. Its larger body also provided more meat.

The Appeal of Being Remote

B y the mid-nineteenth century, as urban centers like nearby Providence and Fall River were becoming dense commercial and industrial centers of wealth, Little Compton retained its provincial charm. As cities grew larger, increasing numbers of their residents sought retreat from busy inner-city life and visited the country, parks and seashore. In summer, they escaped the cities. Those who could afford the expense bought or built country cottages in suburban or rural settings, others of more modest means traveled to resort hotels or roomed with rural families and still others took advantage of public transportation, making day trips for picnics or shore dinners.

Little Compton's beautiful pastoral, tranquil and isolated setting attracted summer visitors as early as the 1850s. Indeed, it was the isolation and slow pace of the area that attracted summer residents. The summer residents, drawn to and appreciative of this isolated and charming environment, nevertheless initiated changes to the town's physical character continuing well into the twentieth century.

The town's emergence as a place to enjoy a peaceful summer retreat did not directly conflict with established patterns of land use. The open, picturesque landscape, so aptly illustrated in Burleigh paintings of the period, still remains the town's principal attraction.

The changes imposed on Little Compton by summer visitors are related to the types of visitors it attracted. Short-term and day-trippers encouraged development of hotels and dinner halls, no longer existing; these sprang

The passenger and cargo steam ferry *Awashonks*. *Courtesy of Russell J. DeSimone.*

The steam ferry *Queen City* made a daily run from Providence, with stops at Bristol Ferry, Portsmouth, Howland's Ferry at Stone Bridge, Fogland and S'connet Point. Postcard, circa 1915.

up around S'connet Point as enterprises encouraged by passenger ferryboat captains. Long-term summer residents lived in houses throughout the town rather than concentrating on one or two locations. Unlike Newport and Narragansett, Little Compton never developed into a high-society resort with a geographic focus on summer activities of the gentry.

By the late 1800s, the Sakonnet Steamboat Corporation's ferries (the *Queen City* and the *Awashonks*) made daily summer round trips from Providence to S'connet Point. The increased summer ferry traffic was well served by the S'connet Point Lighthouse, erected in 1883–84. The steamship company also operated the shore dining hall located at the Point and, in 1887, built the large Sakonnet Inn, a two-and-a-half-story shingled building with a large wraparound porch. Few traces remain of Little Compton's earliest summer colony; a century of tropical storms and hurricanes devastated the wood-frame shanties and cottages.

David Sisson (1803–1874) built his Stone House at 122 Sakonnet Point Road. The land the house stands on was the site of a British raid during the Revolution. In the early nineteenth century, it was the Rotch Farm. Sisson bought the land in 1853 and built the house as his residence in 1854 in the Italianate style. His son, Henry Tillinghast Sisson, acquired the property in 1857. In the late 1870s, H.T. Sisson planned to use the house and land as a summer resort. It is unclear if H.T.S. ever accomplished that plan. Damaged

David Sisson's Stone House, built circa 1854, is seen here abandoned and run-down in about 1930.

by the 1938 hurricane, the long-abandoned Sakonnet House, now restored to its former nineteenth-century splendor, is welcoming a new generation of summer guests.

The presence of summer residents brought about many far-reaching changes to the town. Like other Rhode Island seaside vacation spots, Little Compton's shore drew landlocked out-of-state people. Many of the town's summer residents lived in Providence, New Bedford or Fall River. Many summer visitors are descendants of Little Compton families returning to their roots for a few summer weeks or months. Construction of identifiable summer houses began in about 1880. These summer retreats were not constructed in adjacent clusters, as they were located to exploit the town's pastoral charm, fine vistas or proximity to the ocean.

WARREN'S POINT

Visitors from New York and farther west built the earliest summer homes on Warren's Point. The first of these, the Alden House (circa 1886) at 10 Atlantic Avenue, is on land divided from the Kempton Farm, which included much of the land at Warren's Point. Deed restrictions guaranteed purchasers of house lots certain rights and limitations. An ensured right of passage overland to Warren's Point Beach included a prohibition of selling alcoholic beverages. Such restrictions ensured the creation of a quiet residential summer colony. The Alden family encouraged their friends and family members to join them at Warren's Point, and by 1915, a number of large shingled houses overlooking the Atlantic Ocean had been built.

The informal development of Warren's Point as a summer colony, beginning in the late 1880s, encouraged the first and largest of the town's speculative real estate development schemes. Largely unrealized, Henry T. Sisson's Seaconnet Park of 1895 extended east from the Sakonnet River to beyond Long Pond and north from the Atlantic Ocean to beyond Sakonnet Point Road. It included several hundred lots arranged in a grid along Long Pond and Round Pond, renamed Lake Louise and Lake May, respectively. Sisson also imposed restrictions on the deeds to his developments. Within one year, buyers had to erect a "private family" dwelling costing not less that $3,000 and the building had to be more than fifteen feet from any road. The prohibitions include restrictions on engaging in manufacturing or public trading, selling liquor or building barns, privies, outbuildings, fences, bowling alleys, "flying horses," merry-go-rounds or public amusements. Bathhouses and boathouses on ocean and pond shores were allowed only by permission of the board of managers, and "lewdness, prostitution, and illegal gaming" were strictly prohibited.

Sisson's restrictions reveal an awareness that Little Compton had a special appeal as a summer vacation location and that a concerted attempt was made to avoid the vulgar atmosphere associated with day-trip seaside developments here near the shore dinner hall at S'connet Point. Only a few houses were built at first, and these principally in the second and third decades of the twentieth century.

Little Compton's summer residents introduced a formally planned, self-conscious aesthetic order to the town's physical character. In the Warren's Point/S'connet Point area, builders were restricted to no more than one dwelling per lot, with necessary outbuildings at a cost of no less than $5,000. Thus, wealthy newcomers introduced contemporary ideas in architecture and landscape designs to their vacation homes. Until the late nineteenth century, Little Compton residential architecture remained in the local vernacular, responding to tradition and need rather than a refined nouveau aesthetic.

The new aesthetic vision is by no means at odds with existing rural landscape and architecture. The forms of contemporary residential architecture draw heavily on the forms of colonial New England: richly textured structures with weathered shingles, massive stone and brick chimneys and leaded glass windows with small panes.

Summer residential architecture is decidedly different from year-round dwellings. Summer homes introduce nonlocal forms—conscious architect-designed forms. Summer houses look different because they are different. Their use is not as shelter for a year-round working farm family. They are designed for leisure and for use only during warm summer months. Cognizant design of summer houses plays an important role in the look of the town's individual houses, as well as in the development of a strong Little Compton aesthetic.

The earliest Little Compton summer houses are commodious shingled structures. For instance, the Alden, Clough and Winter Houses at Warren's Point and the Slicer House on West Main Road are two- and two-and-a-half-story dwellings with wide verandas, providing a transition between indoor and outdoor living.

Little Compton's development as a place for wealthy and working-class people to get away from city heat between the 1880s and the mid-1940s added an important new building type to the town. The summer houses built here during these years reflect national architectural trends as they adapted to the specific needs of Little Compton's summer residents. Unlike the elaborate "cottages" built across the bay in Newport, they were never ostentatious or formal; they reflect a strong sense of place in their relation to the town's past and its rural character.

S'CONNET POINT

For many generations, beginning in about 1887, the Seaconnet Steamboat Company ran the ferry service that supplied a valuable link to eastern Rhode Island markets for Little Compton farmers and commercial fishermen. The daily run from Providence by the steamer ferries *Awashonks*, *Islander* and *Queen City* carried passengers and produce. The day-trip passengers, after enjoying a smooth voyage down the Sakonnet River to S'connet Point, feasted at a shore dining hall or spent a fleeting few hours

Daily visitors to S'connet Point promenade the boardwalk, dine and dance in the nearby "casino."

Seen in this circa 1907 photo is the Rhode Island Sound steam ferry the *Favorite* at the S'connet Point steamer landing, as well as its fish processing buildings. The dining pavilion is the building in the background with the flag flying.

The 106-foot steam ferry *Islander*, circa 1914. Beginning in 1886, Captain Horatio N. Wilcox operated the *Islander* and the *Dolphin*, making calls at Bristol Ferry, Stone Bridge, Newtown and Fogland. Captain Julius A. Pettey and partners organized the Sakonnet Steamboat Company, imitating their service with the 92-foot *Queen City* and later adding the 107-foot *Awashonks*. By 1915, only the *Islander*, owned by Philip W. Almy, made the Providence–Sakonnet run. Almy also owned the dining pavilion at S'connet Point; a round-trip ticket on the ferry entitled the bearer to a shore dinner.

at a nearby beach. While passengers took pleasure in the pure ocean air, dockhands loaded barrels of fish and sacks of farm produce for the return trip to Providence markets.

During the few months of the fishing season, the shanties of the fishing village, near the breakwater, housed the 150 or so men who operated about seventy seining boats and trawlers. The seasonal catch consisted mostly of scup, tautog, rockfish, pollock and bluefish. The record catch for 1865 amounted to 310,000 pounds. The reported market value of scup for the 1865 season was $160,000. A dwindling catch in several subsequent years, caused by overharvesting, considerably reduced the average market value.

The hurricane of September 21, 1938, swept S'connet Point clean of all its buildings. All the elements that made this area a typical seaside village—the Sakonnet Inn, the Fo'c's'le Restaurant, the fish markets, the shore dining halls and the assorted stores—were swept away. This natural catastrophe forever changed the role and face of the town's summer life. Except for the restaurant and fishing-related structures, property owners chose not to rebuild; this suggests that the ferry captain's day excursions and the hotel phase of the Point's summer life had come to a sad end.

When local residents attempted to have the S'connet Point breakwater enlarged and extended, their requests were turned down because, according to state authorities, "not enough boats use the harbor to justify the expense." That reasoning did not sit well with the locals; they continued to pressure legislators until the desired improvements gained approval.

With the breakwater now raised and extended to eight hundred feet in length and the harbor dredged to eight feet, the harbor is a far better refuge than it was and a better port for commercial fishermen, yachts and small sunfish sailors.

THE POTATO BOAT

The following is an excerpt from a series of monographs by David Patten.

There she was, clothed in steam and early morning mist, at her berth just inside the S'connet breakwater—the little steamer [the] *Queen City*. It was late August and it was mostly potatoes she was taking aboard for the run up to Providence.

Cap'n Walter Scott Gray came wallowing down the wharf…Already the five-minute warning bell on the freight shed had rung. Ernest Manchester, the postmaster, reached the mail up to the purser, Cap'n Gray rang three bells and the bowels of the *Queen* began to rumble. The hawser screeched at the capstan as she backed away, the gulls swirling up from the breakwater screeching back, she squared away, and with three blasts from her whistle, 200 barrels of S'connet potatoes began their voyage.

The *Queen* lurched and pitched through the cross seas piling in from the ocean. Off the tip of Old Bull Ledge the bell buoy said Good Morning to her, then she passed Church's Point and settled into the smoother passage up river. As she rounded Fogland, the fishermen's wives were hanging out their washing and in five minutes, she tied up at Pierce's Wharf.

There they were, the lean and hungry Yanks of the Tiverton Four Corners district, and their wagons and worn-down nags and spiritless dogs. But mostly potatoes. Potatoes filled the foredeck and every foot of room in engine room and galley.

Finally the *Queen* got away—a half hour late. The Cap'n laid a course across the river to Newtown on the Portsmouth shore. Squinting ahead with his salt-smitten eyes, he saw more potatoes—many more potatoes.

"Goramighty," he gargled.

More scrawny Yanks with their teams, more dogs, but over and above all potatoes, potatoes.

Up they poured to the passenger deck. Barrels mounted on barrels. They forced the passengers back into the cabin, and even there the potatoes outflanked and encircled and all but overran them.

One hour late now, the *Queen* whistled for the draw of Stone Bridge. The draw opened with a rattle in its throat. It was narrow and the tide was running strongly out. Cap'n Gray spat and rang for full speed ahead. Black smoke poured from the stack, the *Queen* bucked the tide. She slatted against one side of the draw. She bounded off and slatted the other side.

The barrels winced, the potatoes jumped. The dowager's hat swished sidewise on her head and a brownish spray from the pilothouse speckled the lee'ard side of the bridge. The *Queen* buckled and fell back. She got the bone in her teeth and inch by inch fought her way through. Then she cleaved the smooth water of the basin and came to rest at Humphrey's Wharf in Tiverton.

She was an hour and a half when she pulled out. She rounded Common Fence Point, shed upon the Bristol Light the full, rich earthy odour of potatoes, slanted into the Providence River at Conimicut. As she wound her way up the channel she left a thin, chocolate-colored strand in her sudsy wake. The men on the Point Street draw knew her ways and kept to the wind'ard side. She whistled for her landing and wearily snugged herself against the wharf at the foot of Planet Street.

Potatoes, potatoes, potatoes poured ashore. Drays, drays marked "Tourtellot" loaded them up and pulled away. Finally, a passageway was cleared from the cabin to the gangplank. In single file, the passengers descended to the wharf.

The billowy dowager shook her finger. "Captain Gray," she said, "you have lost us all our connections. You and your potatoes! Every last connection. Do you think that is nice?"

The Cap'n shifted his lump [of chew] from left cheek to right. As if defying a host of troubles, he brought them to a point on his tongue and cast them in an amber tinted surf that broke on the corner of the freight house like the troubled seas of a S'connet sou'easter.

S'CONNET LIGHT

To the east off S'connet Point, there are several islands and many threatening rocks, so the mariners give these waters a wide berth. These menacing waters were the reason for the planned construction of the S'connet Point Lighthouse. The original plan placed the lighthouse tower on a rocky base northwest of West Island, largest of the outlying islands. However, the plan was squelched because of the influence of prestigious members of the West Island Fishing Club, of which President Grover Cleveland was once a member. The complaint alleged that the lighthouse would spoil the view from the clubhouse.

Eventually, the lighthouse was built (1881–84) on a rocky shoal separated from West Island; for seventy years, the light acted as a valuable navigation aid for mariners. The structure is a white conical tower built of brick and iron on a brown cylindrical pier, footed on Little Cormorant Rock at the western end of S'connet Point, east of the Sakonnet River.

After a battering by Hurricane Carol in 1954, the forty-eight-foot tower of steel and masonry was declared structurally unsafe, and the Coast Guard extinguished the light. In place of the light, three bell buoys and a whistle were installed as warning devices.

The S'connet Point Lighthouse (1883–84), circa 1956. A crusade to restore and relight the beacon began in 1961 due to the initiative of Carl and Carolyn W. Haffenreffer. The official relighting ceremony took place at dusk from Lloyd's Beach on Saturday, March 22, 1997.

The crusade to rekindle the beacon began in 1961, when Carl W. and Carolyn Haffenreffer purchased the lighthouse at auction for $2,300. Now fully restored by a group of volunteers, the S'connet Point Lighthouse is maintained as a historic landmark. The fixed white light is sixty-eight feet above the sea. When active, it flashes three red lights every sixty seconds. The official relighting ceremony took place at dusk at Lloyd's Beach on Saturday, March 22, 1997.

THE SAKONNET YACHT CLUB AT S'CONNET POINT

John Alden, Edward Brayton, Howard Huntoon and others founded the Sakonnet Yacht Club in 1937. An old barn sitting on the land end of a new dock became the clubhouse. Sadly, the surprise hurricane of 1938 washed

The snug S'connet Point Harbor. The yacht club is in the upper left of this image; the club's dock is easily seen jutting out into the harbor.

A mid-1950 postcard image of the S'Connet Point Yacht Club.

away the clubhouse, but the dock survived. Undaunted by their bad luck, the members built a new clubhouse, which became a victim of the 1944 hurricane that splintered the building, washing it up the Sakonnet River. Once again, members built another clubhouse, only to lose it to Hurricane Carol in 1954. With crossed fingers, members built what they hope is a hurricane-proof clubhouse high up on deeply sunk pilings.

Because S'connet Point shoots into the Atlantic Ocean, when mariners leave the harbor and sail in any direction but north up the Sakonnet River, they are putting to sea.

Sydney Richmond Burleigh, Artist

B. Little Compton 1853, d. Providence 1929. Prolific painter, water colors, oils and Rafaelli colors. Member Providence Art Club 1888–1929; President, 1915–1921; first president of the Rhode Island Water Color Club.
—Angell's Lane: Index of Rhode Island Artists Up to 1900

Sheltered by a lean-to on the north side of the Little Compton Historical Society barn is Sydney Burleigh's studio, called Peggotty. In about 1906, Burleigh salvaged a derelict catboat once used as a ferry from Little Compton to Middletown. Abandoned for several years, Burleigh hauled the old boat to his garden, where he built a superstructure, thatched it and named it.

For most of his career, Burleigh lived and worked in Providence, but he maintained a home and his Peggoty studio on the Sakonnet shore. After 1890, he devoted more time to painting Little Compton's rural charm and working farms. The artist's talents took many forms, including designing, carving and painting furniture, making jewelry and designing interiors.

Burleigh's mother's family was among the area's early settlers; his father was a fisherman and a poet of some note. Burleigh received his early education in Little Compton's public school system and his advanced education at the Schofield School in Providence. After a three-year stint as a craftsman at Brown and Sharpe Manufacturing Company, he devoted his time to drawing and painting; he set up his Providence studio in 1876.

Burleigh's Fleur de Lis studio, now part of the Providence Art Club's complex of buildings. This is a reproduction of a pencil drawing by Helen Mason Gross.

Recognizing his need for serious art study, he traveled to Europe, settling in Paris. In Paris, he studied painting under the tutelage of Jean-Paul Laurens.

Upon his return to Rhode Island in the spring of 1880, Burleigh became an active member of the newly formed Providence Art Club, founded for the study, exhibition and sale of art. As a lifelong commitment, he remained a leader in the art club. In 1887, he became a member of the board of directors of the newly founded Rhode Island School of Design and its Museum of Art, a position he held until 1893.

Perhaps his most visible contribution to the arts in Providence is the studio he built on Thomas Street in 1885. The building, called the Fleur de Lis, still stands and is now part of the art club. The half-timber building with carved beams and Arts and Crafts plaster panels depicting the fine arts on its façade is based on architecture he had seen in Chester, England.

However, especially remembered are his watercolor depictions of rural scenes that he exhibited at the Providence Art Club. His paintings are widely collected in Rhode Island.

A Little Compton Timeline

William S. Lynch originally compiled this chronology in 1975 for the Little Compton Tercentennial.

1629 Plymouth Colony claims land from Plymouth to Sakonnet.

1662 Permission is given to some Plymouth settlers to purchase Sakonnet land from the natives.

1671 Plymouth treaty with Awashonks takes place.

1673 Land is purchased from Awashonks.
    Twenty-nine men from Marshfield and Duxbury form an association of proprietors.
    First land purchasers are William Pabodie, Constant Southworth and Nathaniel Thomas.

1675 First plantation is settled by Benjamin Church.
    King Philip's War takes place.
    One-square-mile reservation south of Taylor's Lane is assigned to Awashonks.

1677 Selection for the site of the Commons takes place.

1681	Proprietors meet at Duxbury and cast lots for shares.
1682	Area is declared a township and named Little Compton.
1683	First officers are elected to General Court. Old Stone Baptist Church is organized.
1686	The town is incorporated.
1690	The Wilbor House is built. The first burial and gravestone appear in Commons, for Jonathon Blackburn.
1692	Governor William Bradford confirms land to proprietors; the land becomes part of Bristol County.
1693	First meetinghouse is built, combines town hall and church.
1696	John Woodman is appointed town clerk.
1697	Eliphalet Adams is the first teacher of religion.
1698	Nathaniel Searies is the first schoolmaster.
1700	Quaker meetinghouse is built.
1701	Richard Billings settles in town as the first minister.
1704	The Indian Church on John Dyer Road is built.
1706	The ferry line from Little Compton to Portsmouth is initiated. Benjamin Church begins dictating his memoir to his son.
1717	Elizabeth Alden Pabodie dies in her ninety-third year.
1718	Benjamin Church dies.

1723   The second meetinghouse is built, for the purpose of religious services only.

1746   Tiverton and Little Compton become part of Rhode Island Colony. The Amicable Congregational Church, an offshoot of the Little Compton congregation, is established in Tiverton.

1750   The first gristmill is built.

1763   Toothos Path is renamed Taylor's Lane.

1775   Sylvester Brownwell joins the Continental army at Bunker Hill.

1776   Little Compton militiamen join forces in the war for independence.

1777   The British frigate HMS *Cerberus* is driven from area waters at Fogland Point.

1778   Patriots sink the HMS *Kingfisher* off Fogland Point.

1790   Rhode Island abolishes the Atlantic slave trade.

1795   A lottery is established for the benefit of Little Compton's Congregational Church.

1798   Little Compton votes approval of the federal constitution.

1820   Methodists build a meetinghouse across from the Congregational church.

1827   Sarah Howdee, last of the "Sogkonate" (Sakonnet) natives, dies.

1830   Ray Palmer writes "My Faith Looks Up to Thee."

1832   The year on the cornerstone of the Congregational Church edifice.

1840   Methodists build a church, Pike's Peak on Commons. (Lynch did not explain this comment. "Pike's Peak" may be a droll reference to the edifice's steeple.)

1843   A debate is held: "Church Resolution v. Slavery."

1844   Dorothea Dix, a noted social reformer, inspects the Little Compton jail.

1846   The Ladies Sociable Aid Society is organized.

1854   Rhode Island Red breed of poultry is introduced.

1870   Manuel Sylvia is the first Portuguese immigrant settler.

1872   The third Methodist meetinghouse is built.
The Congregational church is raised.

1874   The Congregational church steeple is built and installed.

1875   The organization of Odd Fellows builds a meeting hall.

1879   The Free Public Library opens in Little Compton.

1883   The present town hall begins operation.

1884   S'connet Point Lighthouse becomes operational.

1885   The Church of Jesus Christ of Latter-Day Saints (Mormon faith) builds a church in Little Compton.

1887   Seaconnet Steamboat Corporation builds a hotel and dining hall at S'connet Point.

1894   The Grange is organized.

A Little Compton Timeline

1910	The Antone Pinheiro (Pine) family donate land for a Roman Catholic church.
1913	The Village Improvement Society is founded.
1914	The St. Andrew-by-the-Sea chapel is built.
1937	Elizabeth Mason Lloyd gives Wilbour Woods to the town.
1938	Surprise hurricane sends a huge tidal wave up the Sakonnet River, destroying all in its path.
1940	Methodist and Congregational Churches unite, becoming the United Congregational Church.
1944	Another destructive hurricane arrives.
1948	The Saint Catherine of Sienna Church is built and dedicated.
1950	The Our Lady of Fatima Cemetery is established.
1954	The 250th anniversary of the founding of the Congregational Church in Little Compton.
1975	The 300th anniversary of the founding of Little Compton.

GLOSSARY OF WAMPANOAG INDIAN WORDS

Acoaxet: "the land on the other side of the little land."

Apponaug: "roasting place," "eating place" or "feasting place."

Awashonk: female sachem of the Seaconnet Wampanoags.

Chepachet: "place of separation."

Conanicut Island: may have been named for Sachem Canonicus; now Prudence Island.

Copaatneast: "thick woods or brush"; refers to a region south of Adamsville on the Westport River.

Hassanegh: "collar dwelling"; the word was corrupted to "Horseneck."

Kickamuit: "at the spring."

Mashapaug: "the great pond."

Mashtuxet: "reed or grass brook"; now referred to as Allen's Neck.

Masquamskesett: "at the place of the red standing stone"; refers to land on the east side of the Noquochoke River two miles south of Hix Bridge.

Massachaug: "place where rushes grow."

Massachusett: "at the great blue hill."

Massasoit: the peace-loving sachem who befriended Roger Williams.

Metacomet (King Philip): chief sachem of the Wampanoag nation, son of Massasoit.

Munnawhatteaug: "fish that fertilizes."

Nanekumsick: refers to the cedar swamp in the north part of Tiverton.

Noquochoke: "the land at the fork."

Nutuquansott: "the place of fishing by fire."

Paquachuck: "at the loar of open hill."

Paschetest: a swamp in northeast Westport.

Pawtucket: "great falls."

Pawtuxet: "little falls."

Peetskeshuet: east side of the Noquochoke River one mile south of South Westport.

Pettaquamscut: "at the round rock."

Poganset: "at the pond"; the body of water west of Central Village called Devells Pond.

Ponham: the sachem from whom Samuel Gorton bought Shawomet.

Quannachuck: the name for the swamp between Westport Factory and the Watuppa.

Quansett: "at the burnt woods."

Saughkontt (Sakonnet): "the black goose comes."

Shimsuet: an area on east side of the Noquochoke River about one mile south of Hix Bridge.

Squantum: the name of the first Indian to greet the Pilgrims; he acted as a messenger between the English and the Indians.

Wamsutta: King Philip's brother, called Alexander by the English.

Wanamoisett: "good fishing place."

Wapwaysett: "place to cross the water"; an area in Providence now called Weybossett.

Wasontuxett: the name of the region coast side of the Noquochoke River north of Hix Bridge

Watuppa: "they draw water"; the large pond between Westport and Fall River.

Weetamoe: Alexander's wife, female sachem of the Pocasset Wampanoags.

Notes

Preface

1. In researching Tiverton and Little Compton, I found several spellings for the native name for Little Compton: Seaconnet, Sakonnet, Saconet, Sokognate, Saughkonet and S'connet. For this narrative, I use the most commonly used of the spellings, Sakonnet, except in the case of S'connet Point, which is the local Yankee phonetic pronunciation.

Introduction

2. The way I understand it, the king's representatives in England wrote the charter, and it is all the king's men who referred to the Sakonnet River as the Narragansett River.

Tiverton: A Historical Prospective

3. Readers familiar with my America's Cup titles will remember that Weetamoe is the name of a 1930 Herreshoff-built J-boat constructed as an America's Cup defender.
4. "Coasting" refers to shallow-draft sail craft that were able to sail close to the coast carrying passengers or commercial goods.

5. The Nannaquaket Neck Historic District is a residential area bounded by the Sakonnet River in the west and the Quaket River to the north. Nannaquaket Pond to the east is an almost landlocked saltwater pond. The northern end of the Neck was originally the home of Pocasset queen Weetamoe, wife of Alexander, brother of King Philip. Unlike most of Tiverton, which was wooded, the neck included grassland and arable land where the native inhabitants cultivated maize, beans and pumpkins. Weetamoe sold this neck of land to Captain Richard Morris of Portsmouth in 1651.

Architectural and Historical Landmarks

6. Julia Ward Howe (1819–1910) was a suffragist, social reformer and author of "Battle Hymn of the Republic." Howe, a resident of Portsmouth, summered in Newport with others of the intellectual and social elite. She was a Unitarian preacher, lecturer and writer and often preached at the nearby Union Church. She died at her Portsmouth Union Street farm, Oak Glen, in her ninety-first year.

Colonel Barton and the Battle of Rhode Island

7. This is a truly herculean rowing exercise. Though not confirmed in the record, I believe that the whaleboats must have been gaff-rigged, allowing them to sail from Warwick Neck across Narragansett Bay to Aquidneck. When the whaleboats approached a British ship, the sail could be taken down and the muffled oars used.

A House Called Nannaquaket

8. Copy of a letter to the Sisters at St. James Convent, Nannaquaket, Rhode Island, by A. Lincoln Hambly, town clerk, Tiverton, Rhode Island, on December 21, 1936.
9. Ibid.

10. Ibid.

11. Patten, *Seven Church Brothers*.

12. *Nanaquaquet, Home of the Late Captain N.B. Church*.

13. Menu for an eating club named The Elastic Table, from the Reed monograph.

14. Comment made in honor of Captain Nathaniel Boomer Church, at the Lotos Club, New York, from the Reed monograph.

15. Patten, *Seven Church Brothers*.

16. Clipping from unknown newspaper in possession of Mrs. Elizabeth Reed, dated June 17, 1904.

17. Ibid.

18. Elastic Table.

Captain Benjamin Church

19. Metacom was also known as King Philip; his Bristol-based clan, another subtribe of the greater Wampanoag nation, was known as the Pokanoket.

20. For a greater in-depth account of the peasefield encounter, I recommend *King Philip's War* by Eric B. Schultz and Michael J. Tougias.

Adamsville and Spite Tower

21. In the mid-1950s, Manchester's store began operation as a restaurant. A disastrous fire in 2002 destroyed the building; it has never been rebuilt.

22. Samuel Church died in 1815 in an accident at his salt works. His heirs sold the property to four buyers, who retained it until Thaddeus H. Church bought it in 1851. Thaddeus lived in Mobile, Alabama, where he was a cotton merchant. After his death in 1905, the property passed to his niece, Claudia Church Hathaway.

23. Adding to the story of the Rhode Island red is the local belief that Tripp rescued a pair of Asian red roosters from a storm-driven grounded and broken merchant vessel. These birds allegedly became the foundation of the Rhode Island red breed.

BIBLIOGRAPHY

The text, photographs and illustrations for this book are from diverse sources, and every effort was made to identify those sources. Generally, text is derived from vintage and contemporary newspapers, books and magazines. The authors of long sequences of directly quoted text are identified when known; usually, this text is in the public domain.

Blanchard, Fessenden S. *Block Island to Nantucket.* Princeton, NJ: D. Van Nostrand Company, Inc., 1961.

Dunn, Christine. "A Sophisticated, Comfortable Place." *Providence Journal,* December 3, 2006.

East Bay Window, July 24–25, 1974.

Falkner, Leonar. *Capture of the Barefoot General.* New York: American Heritage, August 1960.

Gleeson, Alice Collins. *Colonial Rhode Island.* Pawtucket, RI: Automobile Publishing Company, 1926.

Greene, Welcome Arnold. *Providence Plantations for 250 Years.* Providence, RI: R.A. Reid, 1886.

Haley, John Williams. *The Old Stone History of Rhode Island.* Vol. 2. Providence, RI: Providence Institution for Savings, 1931.

Holland, James J. "How the Four Corners of Puncatest Came to Be." *Old Rhode Island,* March 1995.

Leach, Douglas Edward. *Flintlock and Tomahawk*. New York: Macmillan Company, 1958.

———. *Historic and Architectural Resources of Tiverton*. Providence, RI: self-published, 1983.

Nanaquaquet, Home of the Late Captain N.B. Church. Sales brochure. Providence, RI: Ralph C. Watrous Company, 1916.

Patten, David. *Seven Church Brothers Spread Tiverton's Renown*. Series of articles reprinted in *A Patchwork History of Tiverton, Rhode Island*. N.p., 1976.

Rhode Island Historical Preservation and Heritage Commission. *Historic and Architectural Resources of Little Compton*. Providence, RI: self-published, 1990.

Schultz, Eric B., and Michael J. Tougias. *King Philip's War*. Woodstock, VT: Countryman Press, 1999.

Simpson, Richard V. *Tiverton and Little Compton, Rhode Island*. Mount Pleasant, SC: Arcadia Publishing, 1997.

Wheeler, Lucia Hammond, comp. *Chronicle and Tribute Book*. Providence, RI: Providence Tercentenary Committee, 1956.

Workman, Robert G. *The Eden of America*. Providence: Museum of Art—Rhode Island School of Design, 1986.

ABOUT THE AUTHOR

R ichard V. Simpson is a native Rhode Islander who has always lived within walking distance of Narragansett Bay, first in the Edgewood section of Cranston and then in Bristol, where he has lived since 1960.

A graphic designer by trade, he worked in advertising, printing, display and textile design studios. He designed and built parade floats for Kaiser Aluminum's Bristol plant and the U.S. Navy in Newport, Rhode Island. After retiring in 1996 from a twenty-nine-year federal civil service career with the U.S. Navy Supply Center and Naval Undersea Warfare Center, he began a second career as an author of books on subjects of historical interest in Rhode Island's East Bay, with his principal focus on Bristol. *Tiverton and Little Compton, Rhode Island: Historic Tales of the Outer Plantations* is the eighteenth published title to his credit; it is his third with Tiverton and Little Compton as the subject.

Richard and his wife, Irene, are antique dealers doing business as Bristol Art Exchange. They received their Rhode Island retail sales license in 1970.

Beginning in 1985, Richard acted as a contributing editor for the national monthly *Antiques & Collecting* magazine, in which eighty-five of his articles have appeared. He is now free-lancing antiques articles for *Treasures* magazine.

Bristol's famous Independence Day celebration and parade was Richard's first venture in writing a major history narrative. His 1989 *Independence Day: How the Day Is Celebrated in Bristol, Rhode Island* is the singular authoritative book on the subject; his many anecdotal Fourth of

July articles have appeared in the local *Bristol Phoenix* and the *Providence Journal*. His history of Bristol's Independence Day celebration is the source of a story in the July 1989 *Yankee* magazine and the July 4, 2010 issue of *Parade* magazine.

In 2006, with coauthor Zsolt Orban, Richard produced a forty-minute, three-hundred-year documentary history movie titled *Bristol, Rhode Island: Past Present and Future.*

OTHER BOOKS BY RICHARD V. SIMPSON

Our Lady of Mount Carmel Golden Jubilee, 1917–1967: A History of the Italian-Roman Catholic Church in Bristol, RI (1967)
Independence Day: How the Day Is Celebrated in Bristol, RI (1989)
Old St. Mary's: Mother Church in Bristol, RI, 1869–1994 (1994)
Bristol, Rhode Island: In the Mount Hope Lands of King Philip (1996)
Portsmouth, Rhode Island, Pocasset: Ancestral Lands of the Narragansett (1997)
Tiverton and Little Compton, Rhode Island: Pocasset and Sakonnet (1997)
Tiverton and Little Compton, Rhode Island: Volume II (1998)
Bristol, Rhode Island: The Bristol Renaissance (1998)
America's Cup Yachts: The Rhode Island Connection (1999)
Building the Mosquito Fleet: U.S. Navy's First Torpedo Boats (2001)
Bristol: Montaup to Poppasquash (2002)
Bristol, Rhode Island: A Postcard History (2005)
Narragansett Bay: A Postcard History (2005)
Herreshoff Yachts: Seven Generations (2007)
Historic Bristol: Tales from an Old Rhode Island Seaport (2008)
The America's Cup: Trials and Triumphs (2010)
The Quest for the America's Cup: Sailing to Victory (2012)

www.ingramcontent.com/pod-product-compliance
Lightning Source LLC
Chambersburg PA
CBHW070215190526
45161CB00002B/85